Social Goals and Educational Reform

SOCIAL GOALS and EDUCATIONAL REFORM

American Schools in the Twentieth Century

EDITED BY CHARLES V. WILLIE
AND INABETH MILLER

Contributions to the Study of Education, Number 27

GREENWOOD PRESS

New York • Westport, Connecticut • London

Library of Congress Cataloging-in-Publication Data

Social goals and educational reform.

(Contributions to the study of education,
ISSN 0196-707X ; no. 27)
Bibliography: p.
Includes index.
1. Education–United States–Aims and objectives.
2. Educational sociology–United States. 3. Community
and school–United States. 4. Education and state–
United States. I. Willie, Charles Vert. II. Miller,
Inabeth. III. Series.
LA217.S629 1988   370'.973   88-217
ISBN 0-313-24781-1 (lib. bdg. : alk. paper)

British Library Cataloguing in Publication Data is available.

Library of Congress Catalog Card Number: 88-217
ISBN: 0-313-24781-1
ISSN: 0196-707X

First published in 1988

Greenwood Press, Inc.
88 Post Road West, Westport, Connecticut 06881

Printed in the United States of America

The paper used in this book complies with the
Permanent Paper Standard issued by the National
Information Standards Organization (Z39.48-1984).

10 9 8 7 6 5 4 3 2 1

Copyright Acknowledgments

The editors and publisher gratefully acknowledge permission to use the following
material:

Charles V. Willie, "Leadership Development Programs for Minorities: An
Evaluation," *The Urban Review Journal* 16, no. 4 (1984): 209-17.

Table 5.1 is by Jane Loevinger as adapted in *The Modern American College* (1981)
by A.W. Chickering and Associates, p. 54. Courtesy of Jossey-Bass, Inc., Publishers.

Contents

Preface

Social Goals and Educational Reform gathers up two themes and holds them in creative tension for the contributions they make to education. One theme emphasizes hope and the future and the other, faith and the past. The past is the anchor of stability; the future hoists the sails of change. Change and stability go together. Effective education depends on both.

Change often comes after a crisis that calls into question the stability of the past. Nevertheless, when change has run its course, stability is that for which we all yearn. And the new and different is more acceptable when it is related to the old and familiar. To protect against the tendency to reject the past or to resist the future, this book, in a catalytic way, draws attention to both and to the institutions and individuals that they sustain.

Education is examined as having a two-fold goal of individual enhancement and community advancement—not one or the other but both. Our book, therefore, does not provide a recipe for that old-time education. Neither is learning romanticized as the harbinger of a brave new world. We analyze how education may serve both individuals and institutions, how it links the concerns of dominant and subdominant people of power. We believe education has a better chance of serving all of the people and fulfilling its two-fold goal when it is strongly rooted in the past but can reach toward the future uninhibited.

The book was prepared to help parents and the public as well as professionals and policymakers understand in a more informed way the sources and circumstances of contemporary educational concerns. It does this by presenting education as a complex social structure that defies simplistic solutions. It does this by presenting education as an important social process that has both a past and a future. The book provides an analytical perspective that recognizes educational conflict as creative. Competing theories of education are reviewed as complementary rather than contradictory ideas.

Essentially, this book provides a multidisciplinary perspective on the development of educational policy and practice in the United States during the twentieth century. We are grateful to a host of friends in education throughout the nation who nominated the authors who contributed chapters. The scholars invited to prepare discussions are acknowledged experts in their fields of concentration. They are John B. Williams of Harvard University, Rick Ginsberg of the University of South Carolina, Robert K. Wimpelberg of the University of New Orleans, Michael K. Grady, consultant to the court-appointed Magnet Review Committee in the St. Louis School Desegregation Case, Faith A. Sandler, administrator of the court-appointed Committee on Quality Education in the St. Louis School Desegregation Case, Gail E. Thomas of Texas A & M University, Ann Q. Lynch and Arthur W. Chickering of Memphis State University.

Acknowledged with appreciation is a grant from the Maurice Falk Medical Fund for the preparation of this book. Philip Hallen, president of the fund, was a helpful advisor, and Elizabeth Blake provided expert clerical assistance.

Charles V. Willie

Inabeth Miller

PART ONE

INTRODUCTION

1

An Analytic Perspective for Educational Reform

Charles V. Willie and Inabeth Miller

It is difficult to read aright the signs of the times, to determine whether indeed education today in the United States is better or worse than it was in the past. Some say it is better and others say it is worse. We suspect that part of the difficulty in assessing the status of education is associated with the analytic perspective used. "Race, gender and handicapped status continue as barriers to full participation in education, but they are less significant today as barriers than they have been in the past" (Willie, 1987:13). If one is black or brown (a member of a racial or ethnic minority group), disabled, or female, one may applaud the increased access to education provided by public law. If one is white (a member of the racial majority group), able-bodied, or male, one may perceive an erosion in past educational privileges and prerogatives.

The majority of the members of the National Commission on Excellence in Education were white and male. The National Commission declared that education in this nation is in a "current declining trend" (National Commission, 1983:15). Yet the year the National Commission's report was issued, more than 90 percent of all school-age children (including children of minority and majority populations) were matriculating students, and a majority of these students graduated from high school compared to an earlier generation in which most students dropped out.

In higher education, college-bound blacks as a proportion of black high school graduates increased substantially from 18 to 28 percent. The ratio of women pursuing college degrees rose from 70 to every 100 men less than a decade and a half before the National Commission's report was issued to about 105 to every 100 men the year of the report (U.S. Census Bureau, 1984:160, 162).

It is difficult to understand how an educational system that has provided these increased opportunities for all—and especially for racial and ethnic minorities and women—could be described as in a "declining" state. Clifton Wharton, Jr., who is black and the former chancellor of the State University of New York, said that "in the years since 1970 . . . blacks in higher education have continued to open new frontiers of access." He described their rate of progress as "slow and hard-won." Nevertheless, he said, it has been progress that is "indisputable" (Wharton, 1985:3). The same may be said of the educational achievement of women in recent years.

Thus, a proper understanding of the assessment of education in the United States by the National Commission on Excellence in Education necessarily must consider the social locations of the prevailing number of its members. They were not female nor from racial or ethnic minorities. The proportional participation of white males in education at all levels has declined as the proportional participation of others has increased. Thus, if one uses a self-centered analytic perspective, education in the United States could be interpreted as in a declining state for white males but not for others.

A social justice perspective recognizes that justice for anyone is justice for everyone. Thus, the progress of populations that have been oppressed and left out of the mainstream in the past is progress for all, including the former oppressors.

Our rising expectations of quality in education probably have exceeded our actual accomplishments. When this occurs, there is usually a sense of despair. But feelings of frustration and despair should not be permitted to obscure the genuine achievements in schooling during the past eight to nine decades. Moreover, we know that impatience associated with the progress of reform is heightened when the possibility of complete fulfillment of reform goals is within view. Our nation is experiencing such an impatience as demonstrated by publication of the many different reports on educational reform.

Actually, there is evidence that the quality of education in this nation has improved during the twentieth century. That the improved education is inequitably distributed is without doubt. Nevertheless, there have been variations in improvement for all. The National Institute of Education reported in 1985 that approximately 1,750 school districts had introduced "effective school programs" as a way of upgrading education, particularly in urban areas. A 1986 report of the Census Bureau entitled *How We Live: Then and Now* found that Americans today are better educated than their forebears were. Also, a majority of Americans (55 percent) in a 1986 Gallup survey of public opinion about education rated the performance of public schools at A or B levels; only 5 percent graded schools as failures.

Difficulty in assessing educational outcomes is due not only to our various social locations in the community and our use of self-centered or social justice perspectives, but also to our conception of social progress as linear. E. F. Schumacher has stated that a leading idea of the nineteenth century that still dominates the minds of educated people is the idea of evolution—that higher forms continually develop out of lower forms, as a kind of natural and automatic process. "Evolution takes everything into its stride, not only material phenomena . . . but also mental phenomena. . . . Competition, natural selection, and the survival of the fittest are . . . presented . . . as universal law" (Schumacher, 1973:88-89). The idea of evolution is of value in understanding the physical world, but the true problems of living in society, according to Schumacher, are not problems of linearity but "problems of . . . reconciling opposites" (Schumacher, 1973:98-99).

Out of the concepts of yin and yang, the ancient Chinese built a philosophy that has served them well, according to René Dubos. It is the idea of complementarity that "denotes the logical relation between two concepts which appear mutually exclusive, both of which, nevertheless, have to be used in order to achieve a complete description of reality" (Dubos, 1962:4).

The idea of complementarity is a perspective that can help us assess the various proposals for educational reform. If such proposals deal only with the bright and gifted and not with the dull and slow students, they are incomplete. If the needs and desires of the majority are accommodated in our educational programs while those of minorities are rejected, educational reform will fail. Learning strategies for the able that ignore the disabled are unworthy. K. Patricia Cross has noted that most of the recent reports on school reform show little interest in "slow learners" (Cross, 1984:172).

In their attempt to overcome the complexity of learning in human society, some educational planners have followed the path of reductionism. Some emphasize the self while others emphasize society.

Some cling to the past and others wish for the future. Obviously, self and society are essential. Paul Tillich has observed that "self is self only because it has a world, a structured universe, to which it belongs. . . . Self and world are correlated and so are individualization and participation" (Tillich, 1952:87-88).

René Dubos makes these observations about the past and the future: "Life is history and it can continue only if the new becomes part of the old" (Dubos, 1962:40). A study of working-class white families and working-class black families in the United States revealed that the former have contributed an understanding of the essential function of the past as a manifestation of faith; and the latter have contributed an understanding of the necessary function of the future as a manifestation of hope (Willie, 1985:286). Faith and hope, of course, are necessary and essential in an effectively functioning human community. They complement each other as do self and society.

The reductionism that attempts to limit education to a monistic principle pertaining only to evolution and linearity, or stability and the past, or change and the future, or self and individuation, or society and participation probably will confuse rather than clarify our understanding. Likewise, educational reform proposals that focus on a single population, such as the gifted, or the majority, or the affluent, are probably more harmful than helpful. Any analysis of the purposes and effects of education that ignores mutuality, interdependence, and their complexity is defective. This book invokes the principle of complementarity as a major theme. It recognizes education as living history with a past and future that are connected.

Bertrand Russell reminds us that "education has become part of the struggle for power" (Russell, 1977:145). Before devolving upon the federal government the responsibility of identifying our national interest in education as recommended in the report of the National Commission, the values of the government and alternative structures for defining the public interest should be examined. In the examination, Russell's queries should be answered—whether "the State will . . . place the interests of the child before its own interest," and "whether there is any possibility of a state whose interests, where education is concerned, will be approximately identical to those of the children" (Russell, 1977:145). To the extent that a single institutional system is permitted to define the public interest in education, the possibility is increased that education will fulfill a limited but preeminent value that is consonant with the functions of the defining institution. We suspect that part of the contemporary debate about educational reform is associated with definitions of the function of education that are too narrow.

A common notion prevails that intelligence is a "general capacity" (Gardner, 1983:ix), and can be cultivated by going "back to basics" —reading, writing, and arithmetic (Elam, 1978:340). Howard Gardner believes otherwise. He states that there are different intelligences and that this is the most "appropriate and comprehensive way of conceptualizing the human cognitive capacities" (Gardner, 1983:xvi). To encompass the realm of human cognition, "it is necessary to include a wider . . . set of competencies." This means that education cannot be restricted to cultivating logical and linguistic abilities only (Gardner, 1983:x).

Concern about the "basics" is insufficient for general reform in education. The role of interpersonal knowledge and intrapersonal forms of understanding must loom much larger, according to Gardner. In summary, there are "frames of mind" rather than a general capacity called intelligence (Gardner, 1983:xvi, 337). Education that cultivates multiple intelligences cannot limit itself to a single preeminent purpose such as helping the nation maintain its competitive superiority in the marketplace. Actually, a good education, a comprehensive education should help people learn from failure as well as from success, keep in focus the value of cooperation as well as competition, have due regard for the past and the future, and enhance individuals while advancing institutions.

We tend to think of educational reform as a pendulum that swings in one direction and then corrects itself by swinging in the opposite direction. This mechanical view of social change has contributed to both advocacy and cynicism regarding innovations in education— advocacy in that people uphold new ideas as better than the old (as the new swing of the pendulum) and cynicism because those who believe in the old ideas dismiss the new as fads that will fade away as the pendulum swings back.

An analytic perspective more appropriate for understanding education reform is the theory of complementarity (Willie, 1983:255-70). It assumes that all knowledge is partial. Thus, neither old nor new ideas alone are sufficient. This theory is based, in part, on a dialectical concept of social organization in which there always are more powerful and less powerful groups of people who have old and new ideas about education and other essential activities in society. The dialectical concept recognizes the essentiality of the principle of difference (Rawls, 1971:101).

According to the principle of difference, there is no intrinsic value in dominant or subdominant status in society. In *A Theory of Justice*, Rawls argues that no individual merits greater natural capacity or deserves a more favorable starting place than any other. Yet these distinctions do not have to be eliminated to achieve fairness. Rawls believes that the basic structure can be arranged so that these contingencies work for the good of the least fortunate. This happens when more powerful groups recognize their obligation to give compensating advantages to less powerful groups as a way of encouraging their continued participation in social organizations (Rawls, 1971:101-4). The presence of different groups in an educational system contributes to its capacity to self-correct.

It does not matter which power group advocates the new or old ideas about education. According to the theory of complementarity, neither group has to abandon or accept completely an old or new idea. When the old idea is understood as the thesis and the new idea as the antithesis, they both are accepted as something of value and are candidates for a synthesis. Unlike some dialectical concepts of social organization, the synthesis, according to the theory of complementarity, is never accepted as the end of change. There is no end of change. The new synthesis immediately becomes a new thesis that is partial and requires an antithesis to be whole, which is achieved by way of synthesis. And so it goes in a never-ending process of social change.

Under conditions of complementarity, the thesis is not replaced by the antithesis as it would be if social change was a mechanical action like a pendulum. Through the process of simultaneity the thesis and the antithesis coexist until they merge into the synthesis (Willie, 1983:268). The process of simultaneity is uniquely human and causes that which is complementary to transcend the mechanical so that both the old and the new can coexist.

Indoctrination and conformity versus *liberation and change* is one set of themes identified in education literature. *Individual enhancement* versus *social advancement* is another set. We emphasize that both components of a set are valid, and that education should be fashioned in the image of both.

As stated by the secretary of education, "all [of the reports], in their own way and from their own vantage point stressed the need to improve and reform American secondary schools" (U.S. Department of Education, 1984:7). They have presented and analyzed the facts. The remaining task is a proper interpretation. To aid in that interpretation, we offer this book and its reviews of the federal statutes and Supreme Court cases that form the legal context for educational access and reform. The major findings of fourteen reports that highlight problems in secondary education are also examined. In addition, this book presents three essays that survey the professional literature in education and related fields pertaining to education for social control and education for personal liberation. Finally, the editors summarize the discussions and offer their conclusions.

In preparing this book, the editors, who together represent different racial, gender, and ethnic categories, deliberately sought scholars who, collectively, would bring a range of perspectives to their tasks. The authors are black and white, male and female, and of varying ages. While most are affiliated with universities, their schools of employment are located in the North and South and are public and private. The authors also represent a range of disciplines, including anthropology, sociology, psychology, political science, educational administration, organizational behavior, and policy analysis. As you will see, our heterogeneous scholars have written from unique perspectives that nevertheless are complementary.

REFERENCES

Cross, K. Patricia. 1984. "The Rising Tide of School Reform Reports." *Phi Delta Kappan* 66 (November): 167-72.

Dubos, René. 1962. *The Torch of Life*. New York: Pocket Books.

Elam, Stanley, M., ed. 1978. *A Decade of Gallup Polls of Attitudes Toward Education, 1969-1978*. Bloomington, Ind.: Phi Delta Kappa.

Gardner, Howard. 1983. *Frames of Mind*. New York: Basic Books.

National Commission on Excellence in Education. 1983. *A Nation at Risk*. Washington, D.C.: Government Printing Office.

Rawls, John. 1971. *A Theory of Justice*. Cambridge, Mass.: Harvard University Press.

Russell, Bertrand. 1977. *Education and the Social Order*. London: Allen and Unwin.

Schumacher, E. F. 1973. *Small is Beautiful*. New York: Harper & Row.

Tillich, Paul. 1952. *The Courage to Be*. New Haven: Yale University Press.

U.S. Census Bureau. 1971. *Statistical Abstract of the United States*. Washington, D.C.: Government Printing Office.

_____. 1984. *Statistical Abstract of the United States*. Washington, D.C.: Government Printing Office.

U.S. Department of Education. 1984. *The Nation Responds*. Washington, D.C.: Government Printing Office.

Wharton, Clifton, Jr. 1985. "Beyond Access: Challenges for the New Generation of Blacks in Higher Education." *The Boule Journal* 49 (Fall): 3-7.

Willie, Charles Vert. 1983. *Race, Ethnicity and Socioeconomic Status*. Dixhill, N.Y.: General Hall.

_____. 1985. *Black and White Families*. Dixhills, N.Y.: General Hall.

_____. 1987. *Effective Education*. Westport, Conn.: Greenwood Press.

PART TWO _____

EVOLUTION OF EDUCATIONAL REFORM

2

The Federal Government and Education: Observations on Equal-Access Decrees, Laws, and Cases

John B. Williams and Charles V. Willie

Brown I (1954) required equal access to public school education for all because, as stated by the Supreme Court, "segregated education is inherently unequal" and violated the "equal protection of the law" clause of the Fourteenth Amendment. In this decision, the courts pioneered a new role for government in public education (Kluger, 1975).

The full force of this finding of liability against school boards that operated segregated systems and in favor of blacks and other ethnic minority plaintiffs was immediately compromised in *Brown II* (1955). By the Court's own language, in *Brown II* the "right" of the black plaintiffs to a desegregated education was downgraded to a "personal interest." "At stake is the personal interest of the plaintiffs in admission to public schools as soon as practicable on a nondiscriminatory basis." Having reduced the rights of black plaintiffs to the status of personal interests, the Supreme Court declared it proper to take into account the "public interest" when fashioning desegregation plans to achieve that which is in the "personal interest" of blacks. The Supreme Court then required the district courts to formulate decrees and orders "because of their proximity to local conditions." The Supreme Court believed not only that district courts "can best perform this judicial appraisal," but that local educational authorities should have "the primary responsibility" for assessing problems and offering desegre-

gation solutions. With the solution to the desegregation problem ultimately assigned to local authorities by *Brown II*, the Supreme Court
stated that district courts could act as review bodies "to consider
whether the action of school authorities constitutes good faith implementation of the governing constitutional principles."

Brown II backed away from forcing school districts to adopt immediate remedies for the past segregation of black schoolchildren. It
allowed unspecified time for district school officials to plan school
desegregation. Thus, a progression of court cases during the 1960s
centered on determining what the *Brown* decisions required school
officials to do, how remedies should be formulated and ultimately
met, and when perceived negative outcomes for others could be taken
into consideration in fashioning a remedy of relief for blacks (Read,
1975).

Implementation of *Brown II* illustrates the strength of the local-
control tradition in American public education. In assigning ultimate
responsibility for formulating desegregation plans and supervising
their implementation to district and local authorities, the Supreme
Court ignored the W. E. B. DuBois study of the Reconstruction period
following the Civil War. He found that "a restoration of education to
local reactionary control" usually resulted in the "cutting off of all
higher training of Negroes from public help" (DuBois, 1969:653).
DuBois concluded that "local control [of the public school system
under Reconstruction] meant . . . racial particularism." He suggested
that "wherever there was retrogression, particularly in Negro schools,
it can be traced to the increased power of the county and district administration" (DuBois, 1969:665).

The Supreme Court, according to historian John Hope Franklin,
was "unequivocal in outlawing segregated public schools" (Franklin,
1967:566). The language of *Brown II*, however, equivocated regarding
how to achieve desegregation. Some of its guidelines regarding the
manner in which relief should be granted were contradictory, particularly the requirement that local educational authorities assume primary responsibility for desegregation planning. Knowledge and understanding of the Reconstruction era experience should have resulted
in different implementation guidelines in *Brown II*.

Essentially, the Supreme Court was acting as a court of last resort
should act in *Brown II*: It established a constitutional principle. It
acted as the ultimate legal authority should not act in *Brown II*: It
became entangled in equity practices. "At issue is a determination of
the kinds of decisions that more appropriately can be handled at one

level or the other. Creative solutions are promoted when appropriate issues and decisions in . . . education are handled at the appropriate governmental level" (Willie, 1984:31). Of government, Robert Axelrod has written that "each level is able to absorb no more than a certain amount of conflict of interest before the disputes at that level become too severe for the democratic process to handle" (Axelrod, 1970:155).

X The fundamental issues in schooling have to do with "equality of access to and participation in educational opportunities, and equity in distribution and use of educational resources" (Willie, 1984:31). The equality issue is an issue of principle, regarding who shall be educated and who shall do the educating. The equity issue is an issue of practice, concerning how to distribute common but limited resources to fulfill the needs of everyone fairly. Issues of practice are handled best by individuals at the local level who must live with the consequences of their wise or foolish actions. Issues of principle are handled best when removed from the possibility of personal entanglement and local influence so that the logic of social action can be discerned and understood. Federal involvement in education forced a substantially expanded definition of who shall be educated in public schools.

All of this is to say that federal government policy pertaining to education is most effective when limited to issues of principle; and local government policy pertaining to education is most effective when it has to do with practice. *Brown I* represented the federal government at its best, hopefully formulating statements of principle regarding equality of access. As Richard Kluger observes, *Brown I* has been assigned "a high place in the literature of liberty" (Kluger, 1975: x). *Brown II* represented the federal government at its worst, becoming entangled in equity practices pertaining to which interests may be balanced against each other in a systemwide school desegregation plan.

Because the Court, a federal agency distant from the local scene, became involved in equity matters, clear principles for implementation of desegregation were not included in *Brown II*. Consequently, "almost 99 percent of the black school children [were] in segregated schools" ten years later (Edelman, 1973:33). According to Marian Wright Edelman, a significant breakthrough in school desegregation did not occur until the federal government set forth clear principles in the Civil Rights Act of 1964 (Edelman, 1973:33).

X X The Civil Rights Act of 1964 was the work of the legislative branch. Since the judicial branch through *Brown II* had become hopelessly entangled in the equity aspects of desegregation implementation and little progress was made in diversifying the nation's schools, clarifying legislative principles were needed. As a result of massive civil rights demonstrations and the assassination of President John F. Kennedy, Preisdent Lyndon Johnson, a former schoolteacher, gave strong support to the Civil Rights Act which became public law in July 1964. The education provisions of the law authorized the attorney general, upon complaint, to file suit against discriminating school districts and authorized the U.S. Office of Education to provide technical and financial assistance to school districts preparing to desegregate (Edelman, 1973:37).

Marian Wright Edelman observes that "the Act put the . . . federal bureaucracy firmly behind school desegregation." However, more was required: "It took the passage of the Elementary and Secondary [Education] Act of 1965 (ESEA) to give the Civil Rights Act . . . the political bite to overcome . . . resistance by infusing major new amounts of federal money into poor . . . school systems" (Edelman, 1973:38).

In 1965 and 1968, the U.S. Office of Education issued uniform school desegregation standards or guidelines. These established a target for full desegregation and were unprecedented. According to Edelman, "the courts had never spelled out what a desegregated school system should look like, and many local districts had adopted the minimum possible method of compliance." (Edelman, 1973:38).

After the executive branch of the federal government had issued clear and precise principles regarding what is necessary to desegregate schools, the judicial branch followed suit in 1968. In clear and unequivocal language, the Supreme Court in *Green* v. *County School Board* set forth this principle: "A desegregation plan that is ineffective must be discontinued and an effective plan must be established." Furthermore, the Court said that such a plan "must be adopted immediately." The Court went on to announce that: "Effective plans must be adopted immediately so that the Fourteenth Amendment requirement of equal protection under the law for black students can be met." This principle clarified the muddled language of *Brown II* regarding how rapidly desegregation had to be achieved, and whether or not racial minority students had a right to a desegregated education or merely had a personal interest that should be accommodated and reconciled with the public interest. School reform is never initiated unilaterally through legislation or court decisions because of the nature and structure of American government. Attempts along these lines by a single government branch would constitute a potential threat to the authority of the other two branches. The so-called "checks and balances" feature of American government stems from the firmly held belief of the eighteenth-century authors of the Constitution that government with unlimited power will inevitably become abusive of citizens' individual rights.

With a clear statement of principles by the federal government, articulated by the judicial, legislative, and executive branches, desegregation action occurred rapidly at the local level: "From 1968 to 1976 segregation between minority groups and whites declined by 50 percent" (Hawley, 1981:146, referring to Karl Taeuber and Franklin D. Wilson).

Before the second half of the twentieth century, the federal government had not fully understood its responsibility to guarantee the principle of equal access. A retrospective analysis will reveal how the federal government had experimented with a range of activities before accepting its primary responsibility of providing equal protection of the law for all regarding their access to education. Also, we shall analyze the direction in which the federal government is tending for the future.

The United States Constitution makes no reference to education, which was reserved to the states. Secondary education in New England began with the Boston Latin School in 1635. By 1647 Massachusetts had enacted into law the Old Deluder Satan Act that required instruction in reading and writing. Subsequently, during the colonial era, all the New England colonies (except Rhode Island) passed similar laws. A Massachusetts law of 1789 legally established the district school system and the district school was made compulsory in 1827 (*Scribner's Desk Dictionary*:210).

The most successful education reform in American history may have been the creation of a nationwide system of free public schools for all youth. The crusade for common schools was led by Horace Mann in Massachusetts, Henry Barnard in Connecticut, John Pierce in Michigan, Samuel Lewis in Ohio, and others. It started before the Civil War and extended over several decades (Cremin, 1961). Many states did not make adequate provision for education until the latter half of the nineteenth century. Public school systems were established in most southern states after the Civil War (DuBois, 1969:637-69).

Many public schools were racially segregated, despite the Civil Rights Act of 1866 which contained provisions barring discrimination in public accommodations. The courts decided that these provisions applied only to state action. In other words, the statute had no impact

18 / John B. Williams and Charles V. Willie

on private discrimination even when it occurred in public situations. The Civil Rights Act of 1875 was more explicit about prohibiting discrimination in places of public accommodation such as inns, public conveyances, theaters, and other places of public amusement. But schools were not prohibited from discriminating against blacks, according to this act which eventually was declared unconstitutional (Larson and McDonald, 1980:143-44, 148).

As the nineteenth century ended, neither the legislative nor the judiciary branches of the federal government saw fit to guarantee equal access to education for blacks and other racial minorities. Finally, in *Plessy* v. *Ferguson* (1896), the Supreme Court declared that separate facilities could be reserved for different racial populations if the facilities were equal. Indeed, the Court justified this decision pertaining to the use of public conveyances by indicating that "the establishment of separate schools for white and colored children has been held to be a valid exercise of the legislative power." The Court noted that Congress had participated in such segregation by "requiring separate schools for colored children in the District of Columbia" at the turn of the century. The Court concluded that neither this action nor the separation of the races in public conveyances was in violation of the Fourteenth Amendment. This would be the official position of the federal government regarding racial segregation until the middle of the twentieth century.

Because the federal government refused to regard the guaranteeing of equal access to education as its responsibility, the legislative branch contented itself during the first quarter of the twentieth century with appropriating funds for local special-interest groups. Congress provided additional funds for the support of agricultural colleges in 1907. This action was a continuation of the support provided through the first and second Morrill acts of the late nineteenth century. Then, through the Smith-Lever Act of 1914, Congress appropriated additional money for cooperative agricultural extension work (Bremner, 1971:1278-80); and the Smith-Hughes Act authorized funds for vocational training in public schools (Bremner, 1971:1280). Federal spending in public education gave disproportionate emphasis to providing schooling for selected student populations. And very little federal funding has gone for curriculum revision, school management improvement, personnel training and recruitment, or other formal and informal aspects of schooling (Timpane, 1978).

By the 1950s, the federal government responded to the increased demands of a technological society and greatly increased its support of scientific education. Such support was channeled through, for example, the National Science Foundation, the Department of Defense, and the National Institutes of Health (*Scribner's Desk Dictionary*:515).

Essentially, both Congress and the states, by their "hands-off" policy, endorsed during the first quarter of the century what has been called "democratic localism." Democratic localism was not concerned with efficiency, organizational rationality, and certainly not with equality of access. Michael Katz said that at its worst "democratic localism was the expression of tyrannical local majorities whose ambition was control and the dominance of their own narrow sectarianism or political bias in the schoolroom" (Katz, 1973:40-41). As Patricia Graham has reminded us, public purposes for education change as society perceives its needs and priorities differently (Graham, 1984:19).

Meanwhile, as the structure of American society grew more complex, the school system needed to become more complex too. No longer could the federal government abdicate its responsibility for equal access to the unbridled excluding prejudices of localities.

A nineteenth-century effort by the federal government to provide access to education was included in the legislation that established the Freedmen's Bureau. Created by an act of Congress in 1865, the bureau was intended to provide a range of services to black individuals who were dislocated by the Civil War. The educational opportunities that it provided were among its most important contributions: eleven colleges and sixty-one normal schools were founded (*Scribner's Desk Dictionary*:249). It has been said that the federal government had to become involved in providing these educational opportunities for black individuals during the final trimester of the nineteenth century because of the "turmoil of Reconstruction" (Bremner, 1971:1260).

The creation of free, compulsory, local public school systems was the substantial contribution of state governments. Compulsory school attendance statutes were enacted in every state. Mississippi in 1916 was the last to pass such a law. After the passage of attendance laws, implementation was slow because few states possessed sufficient administrative capacity to enforce them (Tyack, 1974).

State reform, in general, has been limited because of the strong tradition of local control in American society. Thus, states have tended to delegate responsibility for school decision making to local authorities and municipal governments, believing that they could more adequately and reliably respond to the will and needs of citizens. Such an assumption may be true concerning response to the will and needs of the dominant people of power. But over the years, localities have embraced the interests of subdominants reluctantly and at best only partially. Rather than checking local prejudices, state governments sometimes supported them. For example, after World War I, state legislators in Nebraska tried to ban German and some other foreign languages from public schools "both as languages of instruction and as subjects of special study." But the Supreme Court in 1926 held that this restrictive state statute was unconstitutional (Bremner, 1971:1283).

While the Court, toward the end of the first quarter of this century, was beginning to challenge the narrow focus of democratic localism, especially with reference to what was taught in school, it still would not concern itself with the issue of equal access to schools. In 1927 the Supreme Court in *Gong Lum* v. *Rice* held that Martha Lum, daughter of Gong Lum, a person of Chinese ancestry, could be prohibited from attending schools for white children in Mississippi (Bremner, 1971:1337).

By the 1930s, the National Association for the Advancement of Colored People (NAACP) began to fashion a litigation strategy that was designed to force the federal government to become concerned about who could be educated and to guarantee equal access to a desegregated education as a legal right.

> According to law professor Norman Vierta . . . 1938 was the date when the legal attack on the separate-but-equal doctrine began. Specifically, he referred to the case of *Missouri ex rel Gains* v. *Canada* (1938). In that decision, the U.S. Supreme Court invalidated a plan under which Missouri provided a law school for whites only and financed the legal education of black citizens at out-of-state institutions. The decision was followed in 1950 by *Sweatt* v. *Painter* (1950) [which] . . . held that [a state of Texas] "Negro law school" was constitutionally insufficient if it failed to provide an education equal in both tangible and intangible respects to that offered to whites. . . .
>
> Regarding the legal strategy, the NAACP lawyers believed that the Supreme Court was not ready in the early 1930s to repudiate the doctrine of separate-but-equal. Thus, widespread litigation was undertaken to eliminate the disparities and inequality in financial provision for education of minority children in localities where black teachers, students, and parents were willing to risk economic reprisals and even violence for bringing suit against state and local officers and institutions.
>
> Finally, the *Brown* decision came in 1954. . . . The *Brown* decision had to repudiate the separate-but-equal doctrine, given the evidence on which

the Court had ruled in the *Sweatt* and *McLaurin* cases. . . . In the *Brown* decision of 1954, the legal [principle] had been won. (Willie, 1983:231-33)

The decade from 1954 to 1964 represented this century's zenith of federal government action for protecting the right of equal access to educational opportunities in the United States. Prior to this mid-twentieth century effort, the federal government had done two things: manifested a "hands-off" policy as stated earlier regarding equality of access to education; and catered to special-interest groups such as the agricultural interests in the late nineteenth century through the Morrill acts, and the industrial interests of the early twentieth century through the Smith-Lever Act and the Smith-Hughes Act. The federal government largely was concerned with enhancing the growth and development of the institutional systems with which these interest groups were affiliated.

Before the *Brown* decision, the federal government's major twentieth-century effort promoting individual access to education was the G.I. Bill of Rights, the popular name for the Servicemen's Readjustment Act of 1944. Among other benefits, it provided World War II veterans with tuition and living expenses for up to four years of education (*Scribner's Desk Dictionary*:262). This effort, however, was not universal, being limited largely to males.

The major efforts of the legislative branch of the federal government to enhance educational opportunities during the last half of the nineteenth and the first half of the twentieth century fit a pattern. Essentially, it only acted in response to a crisis—the readjustment of a massive number of blacks dislocated by the Civil War, and the readjustment of a massive number of veterans dislocated by World War II. As the twentieth century approaches its end, there is evidence that the federal government may now be oriented to acting on the merits of the issue of equal access for individuals rather than merely responding to a crisis situation. Such evidence is found in Public Law 94-142, the Education of All Handicapped Children Act, and Section 504 of the Rehabilitation Act. The latter was enacted in 1973 and the former in 1975. P.L. 94-142 makes certain federal funds available to schools that comply with its requirements. Under the Rehabilitation Act federal funds would be cut off from schools that discriminate against the handicapped (Fischer, Schimmel, and Kelly, 1981:273).

When Congress enacted the All Handicapped Children Act, half of the eight million handicapped children in the country "were not receiving an appropriate education" and about one-eighth "were completely excluded from the public school" (Fischer, Schimmel, and

Kelly,1981:273). According to Fischer, Schimmel, and Kelley, "Congress recognized that education remains a state responsibility [but] also acknowledged that federal assistance was necessary to assure equal protection of the law" (Fischer, Schimmel, and Kelly, 1981: 273). The law requires handicapped children to be educated in the "least restrictive educational setting." Beyond providing "equal access," Congress required school systems to provide "support services" and an "individual educational program" for each handicapped child. The test of whether the education provided for handicapped students is "appropriate" is whether or not it is "comparable to that offered the nonhandicapped" (Fischer, Schimmel, and Kelly, 1981:274). In 1980 the needs of handicapped children became the responsibility of the Office of Special Education and Rehabilitative Services within the Department of Education (*Scribner's Desk Dictionary*:274).╳√

Fischer, Schimmel, and Kelly conclude that "in recent years both the Constitution and legislation have been used to gain a significant degree of equality in education for handicapped and for limited-English ability students" (Fischer, Schimmel, and Kelly, 1981:282). With reference to equal access to schools for children of limited English, they mention specifically the assistance rendered by Title VI of the Civil Rights Act of 1964, the Supreme Court decision in *Lau* v. *Nichols* (1974) which required transitional bilingual education for children who cannot benefit from instruction in English, and the Bilingual Education Act of 1974 which also mandates bilingual education for children of limited English. "These developments," they state, "contrast dramatically with our historic attitude of 'swim or sink' toward such students" (Fischer, Schimmel, Kelly, 1981:282).

The state laws that kept handicapped and bilingual children out of school were based on ignorance, prejudice, or finance. While the changes mandated by federal law are in part based on new scientific evidence and other forms of enlightenment, the changes also "are . . . based in part on the civil rights movement of the 1950s and '60s which reverberated throughout the American culture and stimulated [various population groups] to make their claim on the basis of right and not of charity" (Fischer, Schimmel, and Kelly, 1981:269).

Likewise, the women's movement has resulted in the eradication of some but not all inequality, sex stereotyping, and other forms of sex discrimination against females in the public schools. Legal scholars state that "Congress made a significant impact on sex discrimination in schools by enacting Title IX of the Education Amendments of 1972 which prohibits exclusion on the basis of sex persons from any educational programs and activities that receive federal funds (Fischer, Schimmel, and Kelley, 1981:259). Also the Equal Educational Opportunity Act of 1974 prevents compulsory sex-segregated schooling "particularly if it might be constructed to be a vestige of historic patterns of racial segregation" (Fischer, Schimmel, and Kelley, 1981: 262).

Further evidence that the federal government is beginning to offer educational assistance to individuals in general rather than to special-interest groups, and to mobilize assistance before confronting a crisis, is revealed in the Educational Amendments of 1972 (Public Law 92-318). Starting with this law, "the bulk of Federal attention and aid to [higher education] was directed from aid to institutions to aid to students. In . . . 1978, Congress amended Title IV of the Higher Education Act to extend the availability of assistance to middle-income students" (National Center for Educational Statistics, 1979:94). As a result, higher education has become increasingly accessible to all segments of the population. The National Center for Educational Statistics reports that the "Basic Educational Opportunity Grant Program, Guaranteed Student Loan Program, and other Government programs have . . . attracted many students to higher education who otherwise would have found it difficult to finance a college education" (National Center for Educational Statistics, 1983:85).

The federal contribution to revenue for local school systems grew from .3 percent of the total in 1920 to 9.8 percent in 1979. The Elementary and Secondary Education Act of 1965 contained five titles and about ten funding programs. The Elementary and Secondary Education Act of 1978 contained thirteen titles and more than 100 programs. A greater proportion of the total cost of public education was assumed by the federal government during the 1960s and 1970s.

According to the National Center for Educational Statistics, "in 1942 local sources contributed over two-thirds of the total funding [for education]. . . . But by 1978 the proportion of local revenue had dropped to less than half of the total revenues. The State share had increased to 44 percent and the Federal share to 8 percent." (National Center for Educational Statistics, 1979:138).

Trends in the reduction of inequality noted during the second half of the twentieth century have been fostered by the federal government by way of opinions in court cases and public laws by Congress. These trends, however, are not without counter trends.

Marian Wright Edelman dates 1971 as the beginning of the withdrawal of the executive branch of the federal government from active efforts to guarantee equal access to education for all. Stimulated by what she characterizes as "negative presidential leadership," the U.S. House of Representatives adopted three antibusing amendments. In 1972 the Senate also adopted an antibusing measure, which the president signed into law while attacking Congress for not taking stronger action against school desegregation (Edelman, 1973:41). The use of bus transportation has been a way of achieving school desegregation in local districts. Finally, by 1977 the federal government had backed away far enough from requiring equal access to public institutions of higher education that a court case (*Adams* v. *Califano*, 1977) was required to force the executive branch to enforce the law and its own desegregation guidelines.

After its historic *Brown* decision in 1954, the Supreme Court continued to refine its guidelines for the achievement of desegregation and finally set forth a sweeping principle in *Keyes* v. *School District No. 1* (1973). It declared that proof of intentional segregation in a substantial part of a school system is sufficient evidence that the entire system is segregated and, therefore, obligates the preparation and implementation of a districtwide desegregation plan. By 1977, however, the Court pulled back from its *Keyes* principle and declared in *Dayton Board of Education* v. *Brinkman* that where the segregative acts of a school board are not shown to have a systemwide effect, a systemwide remedy cannot be imposed. The Court as well as the Congress and the executive branch contributed to this counter trend away from guaranteeing full and equal access to educational institutions and agencies in the society.

Caroline Hodges Persell observed that "a great deal of what schools do . . . [has] the effect of . . . legitimating the social relations of inequality." She attributed the absence of full equality not so much to "the direct intervention of those in more dominant positions" but to "prevailing educational assumptions [and] structures" (Persell, 1977: 170). The actions of the executive, legislative, and judicial branches of the federal government mentioned above, however, would seem to indicate that they knowingly acted against the principle of equal access and by their actions sentenced the schools to continue functioning as instruments of graded inequality.

Despite attempts to slow down the efforts of the federal government toward guaranteeing equal access to educational opportunities, the favorable trend has not ended. What has been achieved during the final quarter of the twentieth century resulted from the momentum of earlier efforts and not so much because of massive political pressure generated by large social movements. An example of this is the 1983 Supreme Court decision (in the tradition of *Brown I* and the 1964 Civil Rights Act) that permits the Internal Revenue Service to deny tax exemptions to private schools that practice racial discrimination (Newspaper Enterprise Association, 1985:485). By 1980 the United States had achieved a literacy rate of 99 percent and more than half of its adult population had graduated from high school due in part to school desegregation and other equal access efforts (Newspaper Enterprise Association, 1985:594). Despite obstructions here and there, the trend of equal access in education continues.

The federal government, although reluctant to do so during the first half of this century, has had to assume leadership in guaranteeing the principle of equal access in education because most states, the chief educational authorities in our society, have been remote, passive, and inactive on matters of equality and inequality. A consensus among local school leaders in districts across the nation is that state government tended to abandon them in their struggle with desegregation, the most significant educational reform of the twentieth century (Willie, 1984:29).

On the other hand, in the 1970s state governments began to assert themselves toward improving equality in primary and secondary schooling. Disparities in educational resources sometimes grudgingly became a concern of state governments. The history of litigation of school finance cases is widely acknowledged to have begun in the California state court with *Serrano* v. *Priest* (1971), although such federal desegregation cases as *Hobson* v. *Hansen* (1971) touched on this issue too. "State trial courts have explicitly recognized the need for the state to adjust for the varying purchasing power of the education dollar among school districts" (Levin, 1979). Thus, as the federal government has backed away from full commitment to equal access, the states have been required to embrace and implement this principle, particularly with reference to the financing of education. As many as thirty-six states have been involved in school finance cases.

In *San Antonio* v. *Rodriguez* (1973) the Supreme Court ruled that the Constitution does not guarantee education as a fundamental right and left the design of funding local school systems to state discretion. Increasingly "states are overhauling existing financial structures to provide greater equity in educational funding" (National Center for Educational Statistics, 1979:140). More than half of the states have enacted reforms of elementary and secondary education finance structures.

A 1984 survey by the U.S. Department of Education revealed that the states were also beginning to assume responsibility for improved quality of education. State of the State messages delivered by governors in 1984 were dominated by themes about quality education and the "National Conference of States Legislatures reported in . . . 1983 that education . . . ranks at the top of the Nation's domestic agenda" (U.S. Department of Education, 1984:12,15).

New state policies aimed at improving the quality of public education can compromise both federal and state policies for increased equity. For example, many states have instituted standardized testing programs for teachers seeking employment in public school systems. The purpose of the tests is to make sure that teachers possess the academic skills they need to be successful. In many instances, however, testing programs have resulted in a reduction in the number of black teachers available for employment in classrooms increasingly populated by black students (Garibaldi, 1986). In the future, new state policies regarding improved quality will need to be monitored to determine their impact upon equity.

REFERENCES

Axelrod, Robert. 1970. *Conflict of Interest.* Chicago: Markham Press.

Bremner, Robert H., ed. 1971. *Children and Youth in America.* Cambridge, Mass.: Harvard University Press.

Cremin, Laurence A. 1961. *The Transformation of the School.* New York: Vintage Books.

DuBois, W. E. B. 1969. *Black Reconstruction in America 1860-1880.* New York: Atheneum.

Edelman, Marian Wright. 1973. "Southern School Desegregation, 1954-1973." *The Annals* 407 (May 1973): 32-42.

Fischer, Louis; Schimmel, David; and Kelly, Cynthia. 1981. *Teachers and the Law.* New York: Longman.

Franklin, John Hope. 1967. *From Slavery to Freedom.* New York: Alfred A. Knopf.

Garibaldi, Antoine. 1986. *Decline of Teacher Production in Louisiana and Attitudes Toward the Profession.* Atlanta: Southern Education Foundation.

Graham, Patricia A. 1984. "Schools: Cacophony About Practice, Silence About Purpose." *Daedalus* 113, md. 4.

Hawley, Willis D. 1981. "Increasing the Effectiveness of School Desegregation: Lessons from Research." In *Race and Schooling in the City,* edited by Adam Yarmolinsky, L. Liebman, and C. Schelling, pp. 145-62. Cambridge, Mass.: Harvard University Press.

Katz, Michael B. 1973. "From Voluntarism to Bureaucracy in American Education." In *Education in American History*, edited by Michael B. Katz, pp. 38-40. New York: Praeger.

Kluger, Richard. 1975. *Simple Justice*. New York: Random House.

Larson, E. Richard, and McDonald, Laughlin. 1980. *The Rights of Racial Minorities*. New York: Avon Books.

Levin, Betsy A. 1979. "Trends in School Finance Litigation." In *School Finance Reform in the States, 1979*, edited by Allan Odden, Denver, Colo.: Education Commission of the States, July 1979.

National Center for Educational Statistics. 1979. *The Condition of Higher Education*. Washington, D.C.: Government Printing Office.

National Center for Educational Statistics. 1983. *Digest of Educational Statistics 1983-84*. Washington, D.C.: Government Printing Office.

Persell, Caroline Hodges. 1977. *Education and Inequality*. New York: The Free Press.

Read, Frank T. 1975. "Judicial Evolution of the Law of School Integration." *Law and Contemporary Problems* 39 (July): 7-49.

Scribner's Desk Dictionary of American History, "s.v. education."

Timpane, P. Michael, ed. 1978. *The Federal Interest in Funding Schooling*. Cambridge, Mass.: Ballinger.

Tyack, David B. 1974. *The One Best System*. Cambridge, Mass.: Harvard University Press.

U.S. Department of Education. 1984. *The Nation Responds*. Washington, D.C.: Government Printing Office.

Willie, Charles Vert. 1983. "New Learning for Sociology from the Civil Rights Movement." Chap. 4 in *Race, Ethnicity, and Socio-Economic Status*. Dixhill, N.Y.: General Hall.

Willie, Charles Vert. 1984. *School Desegregation Plans That Work*. Westport, Conn.: Greenwood Press.

The World Almanac and Book of Facts 1985. New York: Newspaper Enterprise Association.

3

An Assessment of Twentieth-Century Commission Reports on Educational Reform

Rick Ginsberg and Robert Wimpelberg

Since the mid-nineteenth century, when the United States embarked on the task of providing a common public school education for its youth, there has been an inclination to continually investigate the functioning of this unique institution. The tradition of assessing and reporting on the schools intensified after the turn of the century with the proliferation of more scientific means to explore human behavior and organizational processes. And every decade since, school practices and governance have been scrutinized by local, state, or national investigators.

The reform reports left by the study groups give us a thumbnail history of the role of schooling in American society. We have access through the reports to the chronicle of expectations placed on the schools. By drawing comparisons among reports over time, we can also gain insight into the process of reform. The documents produced by the myriad of school survey teams and national reform commissions encapsulate a kind of institutionalized activity, interesting and revealing in and of itself. It is these two purposes—to explore the social history of schooling and the function of the reform survey—that shape this chapter.

The total number of surveys and proposals for change produced on education during the twentieth century would be difficult to list, much less analyze, in a discussion of this length. We decided to limit the pool of reports to those having a nationwide focus. This criterion elevates the issue of "reform" to a general level beyond the idiosyncracies of local or regional differences. A second basis for selecting reports for the present analysis was schooling level: we only examined reports focusing on the American high school. High schools have received the greatest amount of attention from reformers in this century and, therefore, provide the most continuous source of documentation. Finally, we chose to study reports promulgated by large educational organizations, major foundations, or the federal government, which empaneled teams of "experts" to make or confirm the larger decisions about gathering information, reporting findings, and prescribing recommendations for change. While this limits our investigation by eliminating large numbers of carefully done studies by practitioners and university research faculties, our belief is that the remaining reports more accurately reflect the national condition of reform thinking during the century, and they document a particular kind of investigatory activity.

THE REPORTS CHOSEN AND THE QUESTIONS ASKED OF THEM

We begin our assessment with the Committee of Ten report published by the National Education Association (NEA) in 1893, and conclude with the 1983 report of the National Commission on Excellence in Education, *A Nation at Risk*.[1] In total, we examine fourteen studies distributed with a fair degree of evenness across the nine decades from the 1890s to the 1980s. Where there were multiple studies meeting our criteria of selection in the 1930s and 1940s, we chose single, representative examples. The requirement that a national panel be associated with each reform document removed from consideration such important studies in the 1970s and 1980s as those written by Charles Silberman, James Coleman and associates, John Goodlad, and Theodore Sizer.[2]

In order to analyze the reports that met our selection criteria, we reviewed the secondary sources in which some of the reports have been discussed, and posed a set of open-ended questions that we uniformly applied to each study document. In a few cases we were unable to gather complete answers for our inquiry because of variations in report formats and limitations in the historical record following some reports. Nevertheless, for most of the reports we were able to gather answers to all of the following questions:

- What caused the study to be undertaken?
- Which organization initiated the study?
- Who served on the commission directing the study?
- How was the study conducted?
- Which aspects of schooling were given the most attention in the report?
- What were the principal findings and recommendations in the report?
- What impact did the report have?

In the next section we provide a brief synopsis of each of the fourteen reports, structured according to these seven questions.

FOURTEEN NATIONAL REPORTS, 1893-1983

Report of the Committee of Ten

In 1892 the National Education Association (NEA) appointed a committee to examine secondary school curricula in America. The idea of constituting a committee for this purpose was prompted by a report submitted in 1891 under the chairmanship of James H. Baker, president of the University of Colorado, which focused on requirements for admission to college.

The main goals of the resulting Committee of Ten, called together with Harvard president Charles Eliot as its chair, were to document a seeming lack of uniformity in secondary school programs and college admission requirements and to strive for a formulation of curricula and admission requirements that might bring some harmony to secondary and higher education. Edward Krug, a historian of the development of secondary schooling in America, suggests that four related issues were the impetus for the appointment of the committee: (1) the antagonism between the classical curriculum and more modern academic subjects like science and English literature; (2) the problem of preparing students to meet college requirements; (3) the increasing pressure to include practical subjects, like manual training, to prepare those students who would enter the work world after high school; and (4) the growing concern over having different curricula for college-bound versus noncollege-bound students.[3]

The committee chosen to study these issues included Eliot (Harvard) and college presidents from the universities of Michigan, Colorado, and Missouri, and Vassar College; a professor from Oberlin College; two private secondary school headmasters; one public high school principal; and the U.S. Commissioner of Education. In short, the Committee of Ten was made up of nine white male administrators and one white male professor.

The directors of the NEA allocated a maximum of $2,500 for a set of conferences to be organized by the committee. Eventually, the U.S. Office of Education distributed 30,000 free copies of the committee's final report to educational leaders. The committee initially planned to survey the curricula in 200 American secondary schools. Due to time constraints, only forty curricula were used, and these covered forty subjects being taught. The curricula were collated and nine broad areas of study were found to be common to most of them: Latin, Greek, English, other modern languages, mathematics, the physical sciences, natural history (i.e., the biological sciences), history (including civil government and political economy), and geography. The committee appointed a group of twenty educators for each subject area to hold a conference during which the group would investigate (1) at what age the subject area should be taught, (2) how it should be taught, (3) how achievement in the subject should be tested in the secondary school, and (4) how knowledge in the subject area necessary for college should be assessed. The conference groups were composed of educators from leading colleges, universities, and secondary schools, selected for their geographic representation.

Eventually, the nine conferences submitted reports to the Committee of Ten. The comprehensive committee report was prepared in large part by Eliot, and reflected as much his ideas on secondary education as it did the findings of the conference groups. For example, the Committee of Ten's final report rejected the idea of totally uniform curricula in the secondary school, a position consistent with the elective system Eliot had introduced at Harvard and similar to the curricular formulation Eliot had presented in a speech to the NEA in 1892 entitled "Undesireable and Desireable Uniformity in Schools."[4]

Although a four-year curriculum was strongly recommended for every student without "tracking," the report recommended that secondary schools prepare students for life's work as well as for college. Four possible courses of study were set out—classical, Latin-scientific, modern languages, and English—all containing a basic set of core subjects. The inclusion of core subjects in all courses of study reflected a belief that the kind of academic training necessary for success in college was also necessary for other career paths. Specific to the transition from high school to college, the committee suggested that any student who followed one of the recommended curricula be accepted in college. And as a general precondition for upgrading secondary schooling, the committee recommended that the preparation of teachers be improved.

The impact of the recommendations by the Committee of Ten has been widely debated.[5] Lawrence Cremin asserts that most high schools modified their curricula in line with the committee's report within a decade. He explains, however, that societal changes brought new demands that further altered the needs of students from what the committee understood them to be in 1893.[6]

In 1904 U.S. Commissioner of Education William Torrey Harris, who had been a member of the Committee of Ten, suggested that the report of 1893 had become the model for all secondary schools, public and private.[7] Although Ellwood Cubberley was highly critical of the results, he did conclude that the report lead to considerable uniformity in secondary school courses.[8] In contrast, Edwin Dexter made a close study of curricula used by over eighty schools in 1895 and 1904 to reveal the extent to which the committee's prescriptions were put into practice and found that, although the report directed thought to problems of curriculum, it did not influence to any marked degree the curricula of high schools.[9] Henry Perkinson claims that by 1920 only a minority of high school students followed a program of study similar to that proposed by the committee.[10]

The Cardinal Principles of Secondary Education

Between 1890 and 1910, the secondary school population increased from 203,000 to 900,000 nationwide. In 1913 the NEA established the Commission on the Reorganization of Secondary Education (CRSE). Like the Committee of Ten, the CRSE emerged as a result of a position paper adopted by the NEA. In 1910 Charles Kingsley, an inspector of high schools in Massachusetts and a former mathematics teacher, presented a report to the High School Teachers' Association of New York City entitled "Articulation of High School and College."[11] The NEA adopted the ideas in Kingsley's paper and appointed a "Committee for the Articulation of High School and College" to make recommendations for new patterns of college admission. This committee was absorbed into the NEA's Commission on the Reorganization of Secondary Education with its creation in 1913, and Charles Kingsley was chosen as commission chair. In 1918 the CRSE produced its final report, *The Cardinal Principles of Secondary Education*.[12]

While the content of Kingsley's original paper was one driving force behind the CRSE and its report, the commission also represented a response to sociopolitical trends of the day. The "cult of efficiency" that generated reform in municipal government, private commerce, and industry, also demanded that the "business of schooling" and the "products of schooling" be examined according to principles of social and economic efficiency.[13] Indeed, the CRSE subcommittee on social studies wrote in its final report in 1916 that social efficiency was the keynote of modern education and "all subjects should contribute to this end."[14] The commission also aimed to address social changes such as the newly industrialized and complex economy, the expansion of individuals' leisure time, and the growing diversity among students who were now attending high school.

A new "science of education" was also developing during the early decades of the twentieth century. It placed increasing emphasis on individual differences among students and applied a new knowledge base about child development to a call for continuity of subjects and skill training throughout all grade levels. Finally, "the cult of efficiency" and the new "science of education" converged on the issue of making school learning applicable to life in the "real world."

The CRSE conducted its work much like the Committee of Ten, receiving reports from sixteen subject subcommittees. The major academic subjects studied included ancient languages, modern languages, mathematics, social studies, English, and science. Committees also examined a variety of other areas like music, physical education, home economics, agriculture, and business education. The commission included all the members of the subcommittees. The most intensive work, however, was accomplished by a review committee composed of ten at-large members plus the chairs of the sixteen subject-area subcommittees. This review committee was made up of two university presidents, six professors of education, a normal school principal, a high school principal, several high school supervisors, two secondary school teachers, and the U.S. Commissioner of Education, among others. The review committee received reports from each subject-area subcommittee between 1913 and 1918, when it released its final report.

The Cardinal Principles of Secondary Education, a thirty-two-page document published by the U.S. Bureau of Education, identified several means of preparing students for their duties as citizens, workers, and family members. In its opening sentence, the report proclaimed that "secondary education should be determined by the needs of society to be served, the character of the individuals to be educated, and the knowledge of educational theory and practice available." The major sections of the report dealt with the goals of education in a democracy, the main objectives, and the role of secondary education in achieving these objectives. The objectives of schooling—the manner in which educational systems could respond to their calling in the American society of the early twentieth century—were deemed the most important part of the report and were to be applicable to elementary, secondary, and higher education. There were seven objectives: health, command of fundamental processes, worthy home membership, vocation, citizenship, worthy use of leisure time, and ethical character. The commission advocated that every subject taught in the schools should be organized to contribute to the accomplishment of these central objectives.

Various subject areas were explicitly connected to these seven areas in the text of the report. Fundamental processes, for example, would be learned through studying English and basic language skills; civic education through the study of history, geography, civics, and English; and ethics would be learned through proper instructional methodology, social contacts, aspects of school spirit, student responsibility and initiative. The report also recommended compulsory schooling for all "normal" children for at least eight hours a week, and all normal students were encouraged to stay in high school until age eighteen. A six-and-six division of grade levels among schools was presented, with a further separation of secondary schools into junior and senior divisions. The junior high school years, it was thought, would help students develop vocational choices and explore aptitudes, while the senior years would train them in chosen fields. The report recommended that older pupils be admitted directly to high school and that schools establish committees to assure attainment of the main objectives. The CRSE saw a comprehensive high school as one with a core curriculum (courses to be taken by all pupils), variables depending on vocation, and electives to accommodate special interests.

According to Krug, the report did not arouse limitless discussion.[15] On the one hand, it probably reflected its times well, having little in it that was unique or controversial; on the other hand, the attention it might have gotten in 1918 as a major treatise on educational reform was dissipated by the country's preoccupation with World War I. Nevertheless, in 1928 the Department of Superintendence, an affiliate of the NEA, attempted to gauge the impact of *The Cardinal Principles* on secondary schools.[16] Its survey reported that over half of the 1,228 high school principals contacted claimed that their schools had undertaken some reorganization in line with the report in the previous five years, while over one-fifth had never heard of the report. An appraisal in 1951 offered by a member of the original CRSE review committee noted that the report had received considerable verbal applause, but deplored the fact that most educators had not acted on its recommendations.[17] Historians Lawrence Cremin and R. Freeman Butts have been less concerned with the direct impact of the report than with its conception of a new ideal for the high school—the shift away from a singular emphasis on the academic disciplines toward a new interest in meeting social needs, and the promotion of school programs with something of value for everyone in attendance.[18]

Reports by the Committee on the Orientation of Secondary Education

The great prosperity of the 1920s was followed by the depression of the 1930s. The high school population in 1920 was approximately 2,200,000 students, less than one-third of all youth fourteen to seventeen years of age. By 1930 high school enrollment increased to almost 4,000,000 students, still less than half of the fourteen to sixteen age group. In 1940 enrollment was nearly 6,550,000, representing about two-thirds of all fourteen to sixteen year olds. The ideal of universal education suggested in the 1918 *Cardinal Principles* was moving closer to reality.

The 1930s marked the first of several decades to follow in which multiple national investigatory groups, research committees, and reform commissions took up the simultaneous study of American education in general, and secondary schooling in particular. For example, the Educational Policies Commission, a joint venture of the NEA and its affiliate, the Department of Superintendence, sponsored two studies (reviewed in the next section), undertaken because of their concern with the social role of schools.[19] The NEA's Department of Secondary School Principals conducted studies on "the issues and functions" of secondary schools. The Progressive Education Association completed an eight-year study (also presented in this chapter) that looked at curriculum reform through its Commission on the Relation of Schools to Colleges. It hoped to support a diversification in curricula that might respond to the varied needs of youth. The American Youth Commission prepared a report, "Youth Tell Their Story," presenting students' attitudes on the social and academic conditions of their secondary schools.[20] The shear volume of these studies reflects the concern of the period over social and educational change, and their focus on curricula, student outcomes, and students' needs indicates (1) the emergent role of the high school as a critical institution for the development of human resources in the United States, and (2) the abiding complications inherent in dealing with a diverse student population with a variety of capabilities, problems, and orientations.

The Committee on the Orientation of Secondary Education was appointed in 1932 by the Department of Secondary School Principals of the NEA. The chief project of the committee was to examine the "issues and functions" of education. The department was heavily committed to the ideal of social efficiency, and Thomas Briggs of Teachers College, Columbia University, was appointed committee chairman. Briggs, a firm believer in efficiency ideals, remarked in 1922 that education was a good investment, and the school "just as truly as a manufacturing plant . . . must work up all its raw material so as to make it maximally useful."[21] In keeping with Briggs's personal predispositions, the committee report argued that secondary education had developed no consistent philosophy or standards and was "inefficient and wasteful of public resources." Given the complex social, political, and economic problems of the day, the committee recognized education as a national concern in need of an agreed-upon national policy.

Committee members were appointed by the president of the Department of Secondary School Principals, W. W. Haggard, and set about their work in 1932 to "study and restate the principles of secondary education." The department appropriated $3,000 for a three-year study to which the Carnegie Foundation for the Advancement of Teaching added a grant of $9,000. Most of the department money was not used, but the committee estimated that time and resources donated to the project cost its members and their employers more than $30,000.

The committee was made up of twelve members, three of whom left before the committee completed its work and were replaced. President Haggard selected Briggs and appointed eight other members. The positions held by the twelve original and three replacement members included: public and private secondary school principals (8); professors of secondary education (2); assistant superintendents of high schools (2); a school district superintendent; a state superintendent of education; and a specialist in higher education in the federal Office of Education. Three of these members were also active in the Progressive Education Association, an organization that conducted its own reform studies during this period. As their titles indicate, educational administrators dominated the committee, and their names suggest that all were men. Further, only one member was from the West and another from the South, although the committee claimed to have uniform geographic representation.

After three years of work, the committee issued two reports. "Issues of Secondary Education" was published in 1936, while "Functions of Secondary Education" came out in 1937.[22] The "issues and functions" perspective was accepted in most quarters as a logical way to study secondary schools, and Briggs had warned early in the committee's deliberations against undue optimism about a revolution in secondary education. The committee met for six week-long sessions in remote locations "where there was nothing else to do but work." The committee identified ten "functions" and assigned them to individual members for reports. Time constraints prevented any collective revisions of these reports. The "issues" were also assigned to individual members, but a tentative report was released in time to get committee suggestions, and several elementary education professors were consulted on issues of continuity and articulation before that final report was drafted.

Much of the content of the two final reports had actually been introduced years earlier by Briggs. In the 1929 Seventh Yearbook of the NEA Department of Superintendence entitled *The Articulation of the Units of American Education*, Briggs presented ten issues and ten special functions of secondary education. The Briggs issues and functions were similar to those that found their way into the committee reports.

The 1936 "Issues" report considered areas of tension and controversy: in the organization and direction of curriculum, between vocational and general training, between education to serve society or "democracy" versus education to serve the individual, and between the universal provision of schooling and a more selective approach. In a background statement and section on definitions, it criticized the *Cardinal Principles* for ignoring the importance of social aims and overemphasizing individualism. Based on the final listing of issues, the committee advanced the following recommendations for secondary education:

- universal secondary education;
- differentiated curricula geared to different students' needs as a means of keeping youngsters in school;
- vocational education as a part of the regular school program;
- secondary schools to serve more than just the college preparatory need;
- the preparation of students for social change;

- assistance to students so they could learn how to voice their desire for change.

On the latter point, the committee was unable to reach final agreement about the schools' role as a social critic.

In the functions part of the project, the committee tried to crystallize a philosophy of secondary education and ascribe to high schools a set of responsibilities. It also attempted to furnish criteria for evaluating programs, giving direction to new programs, and making possible a better articulation of programs from elementary through higher education. The committee's report set forth ten functions which, again, appear to be borrowed in large part from Briggs's work of 1929. They also overlapped the ten issues identified in the committee's earlier report. According to the Committee on the Orientation of Secondary Education, the functions of the American secondary school were to:

- integrate students into society;
- base curricula on students' vocational, personal, and social needs;
- articulate curricula so that the activities they prescribed would respond to variations in student ability;
- individualize vocational guidance;
- organize fields of knowledge for relevance beyond gaining admission to college—this included an emphasis on higher-order cognitive skills and homogeneous grouping by ability;
- take account of individual interests as a means of promoting positive attitudes toward continued learning and developing leaders in all fields —here the committee recommended restrictions on electives, free time, and outdoor play;
- give active personal guidance and proper advising after collecting information on students' needs;
- promote individual study and research;
- provide universal general education with gradual differentiation based on abilities and interests;
- retain each student until remaining in school is no longer to the student's benefit.

Critics attacked components of both reports, but saved their strongest rebuttal for the last recommendation in the functions report: that students be eliminated from school when it was apparent that they could no longer profit from being there. How, the critics asked, could the report be so Jacksonian on universal acceptance and admission, yet not insist on universal retention? Practitioners like Superintendent Caverly of Brookline, Massachusetts, criticized the "theoreticians" for giving up on students who have practical difficulties. Others criticized the reports for the triviality of their discussions, what one called "tweedledee-tweedledum issues."[23] According to this objection, there was too much emphasis on social conformity and docility and not enough stress on preparing students to question, criticize, or challenge what they saw around them. In spite of these criticisms, Krug suggests that Briggs's work and personality probably saved the project from being even less interesting or useful, "a warmed-over serving of social efficiency."[24] Briggs at least urged others in the field to focus on educational values rather than just administrative machinery.

Reports of the Educational Policy Commission in the 1930s

The Educational Policy Commission (EPC) was a joint venture of the Department of Superintendence (later called the American Association of School Administrators) and the NEA. Created in 1935, the EPC held its first meeting in 1936 and its last in 1968. The commission worked to respond to the challenges of the 1930s by trying to unify educators through a consensus on key issues. Schools were faced with depression-era budgets caused by declining tax revenues and smaller elementary school enrollments. These conditions, in turn, spawned school closings, teacher firings, and program retrenchments. By studying the situation, the EPC hoped to unify the profession and rally public confidence and support.[25] It issued two major reports in the late 1930s: *The Unique Functions of Education in American Democracy* (1937) and *The Purposes of Education in American Democracy* (1938).[26]

The reports described the mission of the EPC in detail. For example, the *Unique Functions* report listed several social and economic circumstances that required a reevaluation of the schools: the postwar depression, increasing ubranization and industrialization, and the growing dependence of local economies on the national economy. The EPC determined that these and other changes should generate for the schools a new sense of responsibility for the moral and social growth of youth, formerly the province of the family. The schools were also to prepare young adults to contend with the changing work relations that resulted from corporate ownership overshadowing individual ownership, the new knowledge in the social sciences, the changing picture of foreign relations, and the precipitous growth of government.

At its first meeting in 1935, the EPC had eleven members appointed by the NEA and four ex officio members. These numbers were increased to thirteen and five by the time the reports were written. Alexander Stoddard, superintendent in Providence, Rhode Island, was appointed chair. EPC members included the eminent professors Judd of Chicago and Counts of Teachers College, Columbia, President Lotus Coffman of the University of Minnesota, Superintendent John Sexson of Pasadena, California, and Chancellor Frederick M. Hunter of the Oregon State System of Higher Education (who had been superintendent in Oakland, California).

None of these commission members actually wrote the *Unique Functions* report; rather, it was drafted by the historian Charles Beard. The EPC sought Beard's assistance after he met with subcommittees on several occasions and with the commission as a whole. Earlier in the decade, Beard had drafted a statement on reorganizing social studies in the schools as a member of the American Historical Association's Commission on Social Studies in the Schools. The statement, *A Charter for the Social Studies in the Schools*, advanced the idea of attending to the many facets of students' personalities and needs.[27] In the process, Beard focused on the school's role in developing students as unique individuals. Later in the decade, Beard prepared another volume for the Commission on the Social Studies in the Schools, *The Nature of the Social Sciences*.[28] Here, his skepticism about the scientific character of the social sciences came out, as well as his preoccupation with the objectives of instruction. In the acknowledgments of the *Unique Functions* report, Beard was cited as "the man best qualified for the task of scholarship, social insight, and devotion to democratic institutions."

The seven chapters of the *Unique Functions* report took as a central element the democratic foundations of education. In essence, this approach led to a recapitulation and extension of the dominant themes from the efficiency movement now two decades old: that schools should be run by expert professionals who enjoy the widest possible academic freedom. The obligations of the schools, according to the first EPC report, were to develop the mind, spirit, and body of students through social, practical, and fine-arts training in a climate protective of democratic and scientific principles. In this undertaking, school boards and administrators were to become experts in community affairs and public relations in order to understand and resist the threat of undue external influence, whether it came from the prevalent mood of the community or the political maneuvers of partisan politicians. The commission cited Governor Alf Landon and President Franklin Roosevelt in arguing that teachers should not be forced to take loyalty oaths. It proclaimed that "the swings of the popular majority do not affect the validity of the multiplications table" and that "however able political executives and legislatures may be, they can do no more than lay down general principles of educational policy and must entrust specifications to educational authorities."

The commission's second report, *The Purposes of Education in American Democracy*, published in 1938, sought to amplify and extend the seven aims of education laid out in the *Cardinal Principles* report discussed earlier in this chapter. The seven categories of "cardinal principles" were reduced to four purposes of schooling, namely, self-realization, human relations, civic efficiency, and economic competence.

Little has been written about the impact of the two EPC documents. The *Unique Functions* report got some attention, but reactions were mixed. While some critics found it a clear statement on the relation of education to society, others thought it was a shallow restatement of earlier ideas. Edward Krug suggests that the EPC reports may have been out of step with issues beginning to surface in the late 1930s, the most important of which was control of American youth.[29]

Reports of the Progressive Education Association

The Progressive Education Association (PEA) was founded in 1919 to promote child-centered approaches to educational reform. Organized largely through the efforts of an English teacher, Stanwood Cobb, who became the association's first executive secretary, the PEA remained aloof from the larger issues of social, political, and economic influences on students and schools. In fact, John Dewey originally refused to join the organization because of its apolitical doctrines. He changed his mind, however, in 1926 and was named honorary president, replacing Harvard president Charles Eliot in that position. With the onset of the depression, those who called themselves progressive educators could no longer ignore the impact of the country's social realities on the schools. The PEA came to accept Dewey's argument that the growth of the individual and the promotion of participatory democracy were necessary ingredients for fostering better social communities. In pursuit of its mission, the PEA undertook a variety of investigations in the 1930s and 1940s, the most noteworthy of which resulted in the reports, *Reorganizing of Secondary Education* (1934) and *The Eight Year Study* (1942).

In the spirit of similar earlier efforts, the PEA's Commission on Secondary School Curriculum emphasized the individual needs of students. In its 1934 report, *Reorganizing of Secondary Education*, the commission grouped the content of secondary school subject areas around student needs. For example, the resources of the fields of science, social studies, mathematics, language, and literature and art were allocated to four categories of individual human development.

The major project of the PEA during this period was undertaken by its Commission on the Relation of School and College, which revived the discussions of the NEA's Committee of Ten from the 1890s relative to high school preparation and college admissions. On these subjects the commission conducted an eight-year study, culminating in a report with the same title in 1942.

In 1930 the PEA had set up an ad hoc committee on the recommendation of executive board member Wilford M. Aikin, headmaster of a private progressive school in St. Louis.[30] Given the philosophical and curricular differences between traditional and progressive schools, Aiken was concerned about the affects of college admissions requirements on graduates of progressive secondary programs. The fifteen-member ad hoc committee, chaired by Aiken, included Jesse Newton, Harold Rugg, and Goodwin Watson of Teachers College; Superintendent Willard Beatty of Bronxville, New York; and Burton Fowler of Tower Hill School in Wilmington, Delaware. The committee's first action was to ask several colleges if they would participate in an experimental program by accepting students who did not meet the usual entrance requirements.

By the 1940-41 school year, twenty-nine secondary schools or school districts participated. This number included ten public schools or school systems, thirteen private independent schools, and six university laboratory schools. Over the eight years that students would be studied in the project, the commission wanted to determine whether or not the "experimental" students could succeed in college and how well they compared with students accepted from conventional schools. The experimental secondary schools were not given any systematic guidelines for preparing their students for college, but the commission did provide consultants to meet with school faculties to discuss alternatives.

The findings of the study were published in five volumes in 1942.[31] The evaluation matched 1,475 pairs of students, each pair having a traditional school student and an experimental school student. Differences in college performance slightly favored the experimental students on average, and those who came from the more experimental schools fared even better. A subcommittee headed by Ralph Tyler collected other data on variables such as attitudes, student interests, and the like.

Much of the impact of the *Eight Year Study* was no doubt blunted by its publication at the time the United States entered World War II. The commission had spent over $600,000 in grants on the project, a huge sum for the depression period. Unquestionably, the study spurred widespread discussion of curricular practices and reform, a significant part of which broached the issue of a "core curriculum" for high schools. Further, the design and evaluation of such a large-scale project were instructive. Yet, on a visit to each of the experimental schools eight years after the study, Frederick Redefer found that little remained of the programs they had instituted as part of the PEA project.[32]

Education for ALL American Youth

Near the end of World War II in 1944, the Educational Policy Commission—the same organization that had issued the reports on the unique functions and purposes of education in American democracy—published a report entitled *Education for ALL American Youth.* A revised version of this report was released in 1952 to account for postwar changes, and it was distributed in the form of a summary pamphlet by the National Association of Secondary School Principles.[33] According to the report, secondary school education was still in the developmental stage. On the one hand, about half of all students were not completing high school, and many of those attending were not receiving the education they needed. And on the other hand, population expansion and growing parental faith in the schools' contribution to social and economic mobility were swelling actual high school enrollments, bringing a greater diversity of students into schools. While no students could be excluded from high school, success for many of them seemed elusive under conditions of the traditional subject matter and instructional approaches.

The original 1944 version of the report anticipated a postwar period of extended peace with an economic slowdown. Neither of these expectations were to come true. The development of nuclear energy, the deployment of the atomic bomb in the war, and the Soviet Union's emergence as a major power bent on world domination maintained a general sense of tension during the late 1940s. In contrast, the unusual postwar prosperity surprised all who expected a repeat of the depression that followed World War I. The 1952 version of the EPC's report, therefore, was written to sustain the basic concerns raised in 1944 but with three new chapters that took account of the developments from 1945 to 1950.

The first edition was drafted by George Maxwell, then secretary of the EPC. Alexander Stoddard was commission chair. (He had also been chair at the time of the *Unique Functions* and *Purposes* reports published by the EPC in 1937 and 1938). When the second version was released in 1952, James Conant was commission chair.

Education for ALL American Youth highlighted the dual issues of "the security of American institutions and the economic well-being" of the American people. Essential to both interests were "the extension, adoption, and improvement of secondary education." Having identified its mission, the EPC determined that high schools should have a set of common studies that would respond to similarities among students and a program of curricular individualization based on student differences. The report argued that the high school should help all students with choice making, citizenship, family membership, vocational alternatives, physical health needs, and the development of rational thought. Differences among students to which the school was to respond included aptitude, outlook, interests, and personal and mental health. All youth were to enjoy an education that would satisfy their need to enter a socially and personally satisfying occupation, pursue happiness, assume citizenship responsibilities, and appreciate the ethical values of democracy.

The commission drew two kinds of distinctions in playing out the curricular consequences of its ideas. It separated urban from rural schools and early grades (seventh through ninth) from later ones (tenth through twelfth). Both the rural and urban schools were to emphasize common learning areas in the early years of secondary education, with more vocational emphasis and individualization later. Common areas included speech and writing, mastery of scientific facts and mechanical processes, health and physical development, and civic responsibility. This balanced core program for grades seven through nine was aimed at helping students grow in the areas identified in the *Cardinal Principles* report. Grades ten through twelve would take into account individual aspirations in the form of vocational guidance, a greater allowance for electives, and remedial studies.

Like other reports before it, *Education for ALL American Youth* discussed the postsecondary period, recommending "grades 13 and 14" for most youth. For the majority, these years would be devoted to further study in the vocational areas; for those capable and interested, the college and university were recommended. In outlining these advanced years, the report provided "samples of the many different possible solutions to the problem of meeting the educational needs of all American youth." Here, the report ventured into a few areas not commonly discussed in national commission reports, including comments on the special needs of poor, black, and handicapped youth.

Little is known about the effects of this EPC report on American schools. Offering a general reaction to the first version of this report, Hollis Caswell of Teachers College wrote in 1946 that it was "improbable that national or regional committee reports—even such an admirable report as *Education for ALL American Youth*—can be the primary source of actual change." He suggested that change would most likely be accomplished at the school level.[34]

The American High School Today

By the 1950s American society had changed considerably. The percentage of agricultural workers in the work force had declined to about 10 percent, and skilled and semiskilled laborers constituted 35 percent of the total. From 1950 to 1958 alone, professional technical workers increased from 9 percent to 11 percent of all workers. Lead by outspoken critics like Admiral Hyman Rickover, many began to question the "progressive" biases in many comprehensive American high schools. They argued that technical and scientific training had been disregarded in American schools, and the Soviet launching of Sputnik in 1957 seemed to prove their point.

During the 1950s, several large philanthropic foundations began to turn away from their exclusive interest in higher education and became interested in examining other levels of schooling. Even before Sputnik, in 1956 the Carnegie Corporation agreed to support a series of studies on public education to be conducted by James B. Conant, former president of Harvard and then ambassador to West Germany. Conant was to study whether or not comprehensive high schools could adequately provide for the diversity of students who were enrolling in them. Rather than orienting his study to comparisons between American schools and those of other nations, Conant analyzed American high schools in light of their own goals. In his report, *The American High School Today*, Conant asserted that the problems facing American schools could be dealt with immediately, and he offered recommendations to this end that were more specific than those of most previous reports.[35] John Gardner, president of the Carnegie Corporation, who himself was authoring a report for the Rockefeller Fund, suggested in the foreword to *The American High School Today* that when someone like Conant suggests reform can be accomplished, the country should listen.

Conant resigned his ambassadorship to West Germany in 1957 and began the study ten days later. He turned down numerous speaking engagements and prospective board memberships to devote himself full time to the task. To support his work, the Carnegie grant was given to the Educational Testing Service (ETS) of Princeton, New Jersey, to provide logistical services for the project. And Conant had four collaborators—Eugene Youngest, Bernard Miller, Nathaniel Obert, and Reuben Gross—two of whom were former high school administrators.

Along with one or two staff members, Conant visited fifty-five comprehensive high schools in eighteen states. He selected nonsuburban schools for his sample, but excluded schools in the largest cities that had a vocational component in their curriculum. Because of his unscientific and nonrandom sampling procedure, Conant cautioned against generalizing his conclusions too broadly.

Schools in the study were evaluated based on the quality of (1) their general education programs, (2) their elective programs that offered general work skills necessary to enter the work force after graduation, and (3) their college preparatory programs. Judgments were made about the adequacy of instruction in English, social studies, and the nonacademic courses, and data gathered on the numbers of students studying in nonacademic programs and advanced courses in math and the sciences.

The American High School Today presented both general and specific findings and recommendations. In general, the report suggested that academically talented students were not being challenged enough; that small high schools should be eliminated through reorganization; and that the three essential elements for good high schools were devoted, intelligent school board members, strong superintendents, and good principals.

Alongside his general assessments, Conant offered twenty-one more specific recommendations:

- one counselor for every 250-300 students;
- individualized programs for every student with no track labelling;
- general education, to include four years of English, at least three years of social studies, one year of math, one year of science, and at least seven additional courses exclusive of physical education;

- ability grouping subject by subject;
- transcripts to be provided with diplomas;
- half of the time in English courses to be devoted to composition;
- programs to introduce students to vocational opportunities in their region;
- remedial courses for poor readers;
- an academically talented program (for the top 15 percent), including four years of English, four years of math, four years of a foreign language, three years of science, three years of social studies, with about fifteen hours of homework per week;
- special counseling and advanced placement programs for superior students (the top 3 percent);
- inventories by school boards of talented programs to determine if needs are being met;
- school days of 7 or 8 periods including physical education;
- abolishment of class rankings (because they encourage students to choose easy courses);
- the posting of honors lists every marking period;
- developmental reading programs on a voluntary basis;
- tuition-free summer schools;
- foreign languages offered at three or four levels without regard to enrollment;
- ability grouping in sciences;
- social integration in homeroom period;
- heterogeneously grouped American government classes in the twelfth grade.

Directed to school board members and school administrators, the project report quickly became a best seller and provided the impetus for serious debate among educators, parents, and policymakers. Noneducators who approved of Conant's assessments of the American high school found his recommendations to be a clear checklist worth following. Nonetheless, scholars like A. Harry Passow argue that the report brought about relatively little change, other than being fuel for the school consolidation fires that forced the closing of some smaller high schools. Administrators, it seems, could easily argue that the bulk of their school programs were meeting the standards Conant had drawn up.[36]

National Commission on the Reform of Secondary Education

Civil rights, the expansion of First Amendment guarantees for citizens (including students), the questioning of many traditional institutions, and the expansion of the role of the federal government were among the social changes affecting schools in the 1960s. Reflection on the events of this decade and an anticipation of continual social upheaval led to the creation of several study commissions and the issuing of many reform proposals in the early 1970s. Leaders like former U.S. commissioner of education Sidney Marland announced their judgment that the high school was again a troubled institution, destined to face even greater challenges.[37]

As a result of the changes in students' attitudes, the court decisions affecting schools, and the general restlessness of the early 1970s, the Kettering Foundation, through its affiliate, the Institute for the Development of Educational Activities (I/D/E/A), created the National Commission on the Reform of Secondary Education in 1972. The purpose of this commission was to recognize the goals, programs, and structures of secondary education; it had the conscious charge of updating Conant's work on schools in the late 1950s and early 1960s.

The Kettering Commission was composed of twenty-one members, including representatives from professional organizations and PTAs, a state legislator, university administrators, a principal, and a teacher. Six were women. Members were selected after consultations with representatives of important professional organizations. B. Frank Brown, director of the Information and Services Program of the Kettering's I/D/E/A, chaired the commission.

To augment the work of the commission, national panels of teachers, parents, students, principals, and superintendents were established. The commission staff randomly selected 200 persons for membership on the panels, with representation from every state. The panels were surveyed periodically by the commission about various aspects of secondary education. Results of the surveys were compiled and reported to the commission or its subcommittees. Its public document, *The Reform of Secondary Education: A Report to the Public and the Profession*, was issued in 1973.[38]

The Kettering Commission conducted its work through monthly hearings in different sections of the United States. In the process, commission members frequently met with consultants and also visited schools where they interviewed students, teachers, and administrators.

The primary points of inquiry for the commission were the alternatives to the traditional high school curricula and a general definition of goals for all American high schools. In pursuit of these topics, the commission entertained a variety of related subjects such as teacher training, textbooks, counseling services, career education, race relations, funding, technology, credit for life experiences, security and discipline, extracurricular activities, attendance, and supervision. And the commission identified six conditions that seemed to characterize the status and constraints on high schools in the 1970s:

- increased costs with declining enrollments;
- teacher surpluses, coupled with a greater need for the high school to assume the in-service training of teachers;
- the disappointing impact of innovations on the schools;
- the burden of poor attendance, class cutting, and crime;
- the compounding effect of changes in the mission as dictated to the schools from society;
- discussions about "deschooling" society with the end result of eliminating high schools.

The commission proposed a wide array of recommendations, a few of which sounded similar to previous commission proposals, while others were more original products of the period and social context of the schools. With an emphasis on alternatives to accommodate differences among students—an old theme but more fervent in this report than in others—the commission recommended that alternative paths to graduation and wholly alternative schools be provided and that a variety of teaching models be developed in teacher-training institutions; at the same time, it argued that course-exemption credit for life experience should be reassessed. In the spirit of equal opportunity and student rights, the commission wanted biases to be eliminated from texts, affirmed the need for bias-free counseling and nonsexist treatment of students and subject matter, supported affirmative action, called for safeguarding the privacy of student records, and advocated the abolition of corporal punishment and of scholarship criteria for participation in extracurricular activities. Yet it also argued for increased school security, school codes of students' rights and obligations, and control over school newspapers.

No assessments of the impact of the Kettering Commission report have been made, but its proposals drew a variety of comments from observers. Cawelti, for example, concluded that, "although the report is important reading for secondary school principals, it does not afford a much needed new sense of direction for the high school curriculum today."[39] Similarly, Van Til conjectured that the social conditions of the 1970s were the greatest obstacle to the implementation of proposals offered by the Kettering Commission and others of its era.[40]

The Paideia Proposal

The issuance of a raft of reports during the period 1980-83 caused this decade to be dubbed "the decade of the reports" even before it had reached its halfway point. The first notable report was written by the Paideia Group and is known as *The Paideia Proposal*.[41] Led by Mortimer Adler, the Paideia Group undertook a study of schooling for several reasons. Public schools were perceived to be in decline and private school enrollments were mounting; minority students were graduating with skill deficiencies; the work force in general was becoming underskilled, and universities were expanding their remedial programs; discipline problems were thought to be worse than ever; and amid all the complaints about schools, the costs of education were continuing to rise. Adler brought to the group's study of these conditions the philosophical idea that truth is knowable and the ends of education are the same for all persons—such ends relating to absolute and universal principles. *The Paideia Proposal* presents a systematic plan for translating Adler's philosophy into a single high school curriculum. The word, *paideia*, the report explains, refers to general and humanistic learning, the kind that should be the common possession of all human beings.

In addition to Adler, twenty educators were involved in the Paideia project. Among them were a current college president and two former ones, two black school superintendents, Ernest Boyer (the president of the Carnegie Foundation for the Advancement of Teaching), Theodore Sizer, and other representatives from schools, universities, and research institutes. Two of the members were women, and none was an elementary or secondary classroom teacher. The final report, an eighty-four-page document, was published in 1982 and sold in bookstores around the country.

The report outlines three objectives for basic schooling: to provide a child with the opportunity for personal development; to prepare the child to be an intelligent citizen; and to train the child in a nonspecific way as a future wage earner. To achieve these objectives, the Paideia group envisioned schooling as a general and liberal undertaking, with a single twelve-year course of study for all. (The only elective proposed in the report is a second foreign language.)

The Paideia Proposal presents a course of study divided into three divisions or "columns," all of which are deemed essential. The columns contain no specific courses but areas of study. The first column is devoted to subject areas, and three groups of disciplines are recommended: (1) language, literature, and fine arts; (2) mathematics and natural science; and (3) history, geography, and social studies. The second column is devoted to the intellectual skills that make it possible to think clearly and critically. The two major components are language and communication skills (i.e., reading, writing, etc.) and mathematical and scientific skills (i.e., measuring, calculating, etc.). The third column is devoted to enlarging the understanding of ideas and values. The materials in this column are great books and other products of human artistry. The Paideia Group also proposed three adjuncts to the main courses of study, physical education (including hygiene), manual skills (cooking, sewing, operating machines), and an introduction to the world of work.

Each column is associated with a particular form of pedagogy. The first column would employ didactic teaching methods using textbooks and manuals. The skills of the second column would be transmitted through coaching, and the third column would involve Socratic instruction of the seminar format in which students and teacher learn as equals. *The Paideia Proposal* emphasizes the importance of the quality of learning and teaching, as well as the quality of homework. Learning should be an active endeavor for students, and teachers themselves should receive a general/liberal preparation (paideia), coupled with advanced training and supervised clinical experiences—as part of their preparation, teachers were to observe master teachers at work.

The report received the commendation of Albert Shanker, president of the American Federation of Teachers, and was reviewed in the popular press and weekly news magazines. Because of its focused philosophical underpinnings, it stood out among the plethora of commission publications during its time. Its impact on schools, however, appears to be minimal. On the one hand, *The Paideia Proposal*, like others of its vintage, was overshadowed and outpublicized by the government commission report, *A Nation at Risk*, issued a year later. On the other hand, Willis Hawley suggests that this report was destined to be ineffective because "it is an artist's rendering that pays little attention to the practical problems."[42] Hawley sees its core curriculum as unsound and criticizes the Paideia Group for ignoring learning theory and school effectiveness research. Finally, he dismissed the report's emphasis on curricular revisions as inadequate.

Making the Grade

During 1982, a group of trustees for the Twentieth Century Fund urged their staff to consider studying the problems of schools in America. A task force was formed, and it determined that the major problem facing education was its failure to produce youth skilled enough to respond to the growing importance of technology. In its early deliberations, the task force took special note of the work of other commissions doing their own analysis of school problems and found that they were paying too little attention to the role of federal policy and programs in education. As a result, the task force commissioned background papers on the history and the current status of federal involvement in education, the latter of which was written by Paul Peterson, then professor of political science and education at the University of Chicago, who also served as the task force's rapporteur. Peterson's paper was published with the task force's report under the title, *Making the Grade*.[43]

The task force was composed of eleven members. Robert Wood, a former secretary of the Department of Housing and Urban Development, served as its chair. The other ten members included seven university professors—four in education, two in government and public affairs, and one in romance languages—a college president, a county school superintendent, and the department chair at a medical center. Three of the eleven were women. Two of them were also members of the Twentieth Century Fund Board of Trustees who had called for the study to begin with. In its deliberations, the task force met several times with representatives from a number of interested groups, including the National Education Association, the American Federation of Teachers, the National Institute of Education, and the New York City Board of Education.

The final report was composed of two parts: 25 pages of findings and recommendations and Peterson's 135-page background paper, most of which discussed the federal role in education. Given the significant reductions in direct federal aid for categorical programs and the Reagan administration's rationale for them, the report refuted claims that federal government involvement in education is at the heart of current school problems. Indeed, the task force noted several successes of the federal government, including Head Start, Title I of the Elementary and Secondary Education Act of 1965, and other work of the recently established Department of Education. *Making the Grade* also applauded the conscious rhetoric, if not the implementation, of affirmative action in federal education programs. One interesting contradiction between the findings section and Peterson's paper stands out: the report began with the assumption that schools are in trouble, while Peterson's analysis suggests that schools are probably no worse off in 1983 than ever before.

In analyzing current problems in education, *Making the Grade* suggests that demographic changes as well as shifting attitudes toward traditional values overburdened schools, with the outcome that, in 1980, they had larger numbers of students and a larger percentage of problem students than before. The report also determined that external influences such as the increasing prevalence of drugs, weakened family units, and new judicial interventions were affecting schools. From inside, the report criticized the "trade union mentality [among teachers] that has accompanied the bureaucratization and politicization of the schools." Concerning the role of the federal government, the report concludes that "educating the young is a compelling national interest," especially since the federal government "is charged with providing for the security and well-being of our democratic society, which rest largely on a strong and competent system of public education."

As a local remedy, the report recommends to school districts a core curriculum for all students. Reading, writing, calculating, science, foreign languages, civics, and a rudimentary knowledge of computers would make up the core. Recommendations for the federal role varied from its publicizing the need for better schools to serve all young Americans, to setting up a federally funded "master teacher" program, to recognizing and rewarding excellence in teaching (at an estimated five-year cost of $5 billion). The federal government, according to the task force, should also establish literacy in English as the main objective in elementary schools, with funds channeled to non-English-speaking students. Federal support should help train teachers—in particular teachers of foreign languages (so that all students might eventually learn a foreign tongue), and teachers of math and science (because the nation's technical literacy was desperately poor and there were too few teachers in these areas). Federal categorical support for the education of poor and handicapped children should continue or be reinstated, and "impact aid" that had helped districts with military bases should be rerouted to districts with large numbers of immigrant children. The task force advocated a program of federal fellowships for school districts to establish individualized instruction programs in separate facilities for students unable to succeed in traditional settings. And in support of all these federal efforts, it called for data gathering, evaluation, and fundamental research to be sponsored by the Department of Education. Finally, the task force took a position against voucher or tuition tax credit schemes.

While many of the recommendations of *Making the Grade* call for a federal stance reminiscent of the 1960s, the report struck some observers, like Walter Feinberg, as antiegalitarian.[44] On the one hand it argued for a restoration of federal activity, while on the other hand it considered the equity orientation of some earlier federal programs burdensome. Regardless of its internal ideological tensions, *Making the Grade* has the ring of interventionist strategies from earlier decades and is not likely to challenge the mood for federal disengagement that has dominated recent sentiment about government.

High School

In the spring of 1980, the Board of Trustees of the Carnegie Foundation for the Advancement of Teaching met to consider undertaking a study of American education. They believed that high schools had been weakened by reduced financial support, declining public confidence, and a general confusion over goals. The study they decided to commission would be limited to public high schools, and would look at ways to strengthen academic quality and equity by focusing on teachers, students, and the curriculum. Ernest Boyer, president of the foundation, wrote the 350-page report which was subsequently published in 1983 under the title, *High School: A Report on Secondary Education in America.*[45]

To conduct the study, a national panel of twenty-eight members was selected, including principals, superintendents, university administrators and faculty members, parents, school board members, educational consultants, and a few nationally known figures (like Walter Cronkite of CBS News). Ten of the twenty-eight members were women. This panel gave general direction to Boyer and the foundation staff; the specific design and analyses of the investigation were determined by the staff and research consultants they hired. In the end, the panel was not asked to endorse either the conclusions or recommendations that went into the final report.

To help define the issues for investigation, foundation staff members reviewed school research literature, visited schools, and talked to educators. Approximately a dozen leading educators and researchers served as consultants or drafted background papers. From all of this support activity, Boyer considered two recent studies as most helpful to the Carnegie investigation: John Goodlad's research project that was later published as *A Place Called School* and James Coleman's and his associates' study, *High School Achievement*, which provided valuable information on students in 869 public high schools.[46] To gather specific data for the Carnegie study, the Carnegie panel chose fifteen public high schools for closer scrutiny. The schools were geographically dispersed; large and small; urban, suburban, and rural; specialized and comprehensive; rich and poor; homogeneous and racially/culturally mixed. Twenty-five educators (mostly from universities and research institutions) were selected to visit the schools for twenty days, during which they were to make observations and conduct interviews with principals, teachers, students, and parents. Observers also sat in on PTA meetings, pep rallies, and the like. In total, the research teams spent more than 2,000 hours in the fifteen high schools. Vito Perrone, then dean of the School of Teaching and Learning at the University of North Dakota, was the leader of the visitation project. He reviewed the visitation team reports and prepared a synthesis for Boyer and his staff.

The final report is divided into six parts and focuses on nine topics considered critically important: goals, curriculum, teaching, learning, technology, structure, school leadership, connections beyond the campus, and community support. The report concludes by identifying twelve priorities that, together, form an agenda for action. Each high school should clarify its internally shared goals and mission. Its teaching and curriculum should reflect an obligation to help all students become skilled in written and oral English. It should ensure that students move with confidence from high school to work and further education at the same time that it helps them meet their social and civic obligations. For the initial years, all students should be placed on one track and should study a core curriculum consisting of literature, U.S. history, Western civilization, non-Western civilization, science and the natural world, technology, mathematics, foreign language, the arts, health, and civics. In the later years, students could choose from "elective clusters." Boyer's *High School* placed considerable emphasis on problems in instruction (the use of different styles), teaching conditions (career paths), compensation (higher salaries), and teacher preparation. It advocated equal concern for the needs of gifted and remedial students, and it made some of the strongest statements of all the 1980s' reports about the role of the principal, who must be accepted as the local leader, being well prepared with more control over budget, personnel, etc. Boyer called for businesses and colleges to "adopt" and support individual high schools. To specify these priorities, nearly ninety recommendations were proposed.

Given the large number of reports produced in the 1980s, the impact of any single report is difficult to gauge. Boyer's personal prestige and the reputation of the Carnegie Foundation enhance the legitimacy of *High School* as a thoughtfully and carefully constructed reform document. Further, Diane Ravitch suggests that Boyer's having served as U.S. commissioner of education during the Carter administration may have neutralized the partisanship associated with the Reagan Department of Education and its strong interest in school reform.[47] *High School* is among the more widely discussed reports of the 1980s, but there is no evidence to date concerning its impact on school practices.

A Nation at Risk

In 1981 U.S. Secretary of Education T. H. Bell created the National Commission on Excellence in Education (NCEE) and directed it to present a report on the quality of education in America in 1983. The purpose was to help define the problems affecting education and to provide solutions. According to the final report, *A Nation at Risk: The Imperative for Educational Reform*, the commission was created because of Bell's concern about "the widespread public perception that something is seriously remiss in our educational system." The commission was therefore established "to provide leadership, constructive criticism, and effective assistance to schools and universities."

The NCEE was chaired by David Gardner, the president of the University of Utah and president-elect of the University of California, Berkeley. The seventeen other members included three college or university presidents, two university professors (physics and chemistry), two local school board members, two principals, two educational consultants, a state school board member, a superintendent, a former governor, a former state commissioner of education, a retired chairman of a major corporation, and a teacher. Five of the eighteen members were women.

The commission was given six specific charges: to assess the quality of teaching and learning in public and private schools, colleges, and universities; to compare U.S. high schools with those in other advanced nations; to explore the relationships between college admission requirements and high school achievement; to identify programs that result in noticeable student success in college; to assess the degree to which major social and educational changes in the last twenty-five years have affected student achievement; and to define the problems to be overcome if excellence in education is to be achieved.

To gather information for *A Nation at Risk*, the NCEE held eight meetings and conducted a series of public hearings and discussion sessions. It also commissioned forty papers from educational experts and reviewed existing analyses of problems in education, along with descriptions of exemplary programs and approaches. Finally, it took account of letters voluntarily submitted by concerned citizens, teachers, and administrators. With the guidance of Executive Director Milton Goldberg, the commission staff analyzed much of the material and prepared its own reports. The estimated cost for the activities of NCEE members was $332,000 with an additional $453,000 for staff support.

The sixty-five-page manifesto, *A Nation at Risk*, suggests that American education is being eroded by "a rising tide of mediocrity" threatening the nation's future. In fact, the NCEE claimed that "if an unfriendly foreign power had attempted to impose on America the mediocre educational performance that exists today, we might well have viewed it as an act of war." The main risk it identified is that America's position in the world is no longer secure, increasingly jeopardized in business and technology.

Major findings were grouped into the areas of content, expectations, time, and teaching. In *A Nation at Risk*, the NCEE criticized high school curricula as diluted by electives and courses in physical health and remedial subjects. The commission thought that subjects like mathematics, foreign languages, the sciences, and geography were underemphasized, and that teachers assigned too little homework. It concluded that the use of competency tests was excessive, college admissions too open, and textbooks inadequate. American schools were found to spend too little time on classwork and to spend it ineffectively. On the subject of teachers, the commission was alarmed at the poor quality of students entering teaching, the shortage of teachers in math and science, and the quality of preparation programs available to prospective teachers.

Recommendations in *A Nation at Risk* were organized around the major sections in the findings areas—content, standards and expectations, time, teaching—with the addition of recommendations on leadership and fiscal support. In the area of content, the commission called for five "new" basics, including four years of English, three years of mathematics, science, and social studies, and a half year of computer science. It also strongly recommended two years of foreign language for the college bound. In the area of standards and expectations, the report recommended that schools, colleges, and universities adopt more rigorous and measurable standards and raise expectations for performance and student conduct. It also recommended that more time should be allocated to learning the new basics; this would require a more effective use of the existing school day and, perhaps, a longer school day or year.

Concerning teaching, the NCEE proposed higher educational standards for entering the profession, including proven competence in an academic discipline. In return, teachers should get higher, performance-based salaries, eleven-month contracts that incorporated their planning functions, and career ladder possibilities, with a master teacher category for those who could design teacher-preparation courses and supervise novice teachers. The report also called for loans and grants to attract outstanding students to teaching and advised the hiring of qualified individuals with college degrees to work in areas of teacher shortages like science and math.

The last set of recommendations dealing with leadership and fiscal support exhorts citizens to provide better funding and to hold educators and elected officials responsible for reform. The NCEE left the primary responsibility for finance and governance with state and local officials, reserving for the federal government a supporting role in special educational programs for the gifted, disadvantaged, and handicapped. The federal level, it said, should also identify the national interest, collect educational data, and provide financial assistance for students and researchers.

A Nation at Risk clearly helped spur national interest in school reform. Major journals like the *Harvard Educational Review, Phi Delta Kappan,* and *Education and Urban Society* devoted significant space to discussing the report, and major newspapers and other print and electronic media carried excerpts from it.[48] Several hundred state-sponsored studies of schooling followed in its footsteps. Yet the direct effect of *A Nation at Risk* on schools, as opposed to the reform debate, may be limited. Wimpelberg and Ginsberg, for example, found that it had a negligible effect on local school district decision making in one state.[49]

EDUCATIONAL REFORM BY COMMISSION: CONCLUSIONS FROM THE RESEARCH QUESTIONS

Our synopses of the reform reports in the previous section were built around seven analytic questions. We can develop a particular profile of educational history and generalize about the commission process by reviewing the original seven questions, revised here to apply to all fourteen reports collectively.

- What caused the studies to be undertaken?
- Which organizations initiated the studies?
- Who served on the commissions directing the studies?
- How were the studies conducted?
- What aspects of schooling were given the most attention in the reports?
- What were the principal findings and recommendations in the reports?
- What impact did the reports have?

In this concluding section, we compare data on these questions, looking for similarities and differences among the reports, common themes that span the ninety years under review, and historical breaks between the concerns of one period versus another.

What Caused the Studies to Be Undertaken?

The problems the reports addressed make it seem as though American high schools have never fully met the expectations of society. Across the entire period of reports reviewed here, high schools are constantly criticized for not dealing adequately with the diversity of students of secondary school age. The earlier reports express a concern about the number of teenage students who never enrolled in high school; later reports refer to the number of students who dropped out after a year or two; and the most recent reports cite high rates of illiteracy even among high school graduates. A related issue is the articulation between the high school and postsecondary experiences of students, whether they go to college or directly to the workplace. This problem identified by the national commissions carries us full circle, from the Committee of Ten's interest in standardizing college preparatory high school curricula in line with college entrance requirements to the National Commission on Excellence in Education's concern for raising the academic rigor in both high school curricula and college entrance requirements.

After the radical political and economic adjustments that came with World War II, the atomic bomb, and the cold war, the reform reports carried a sense of paradise lost, as though high schools only a decade or two before had enjoyed halcyon days. For example, the NCEE and James Conant echo this theme, yet the glory years that the NCEE wants to reclaim are precisely those with which Conant finds fault.

Of course, it is after World War II that the issue of federal aid enters the discussion. Prior to the war, federal involvement was insignificant. However, the Kettering Commission (National Commission on the Reform of Secondary Education) noted that schools were having to respond to federal judicial intervention on behalf of students' rights and social equity; and we have, to some degree, an ideological argument between the Twentieth Century Fund's task force which created a platform for renewed federal aid and the federal government's National Commission on Excellence in Education which supports federal disengagement in favor of state and local initiative.

Which Organization Initiated the Study?

Since we only selected reports with a national scope promoted by educational organizations, foundations, and the federal government, our conclusions here show little variance. The importance of the National Education Association during the first half of the century, however, is noteworthy. All but one of the documents we analyzed published prior to 1952 were sponsored by the NEA or one of its affiliates. With the growth of teacher collective bargaining in the 1950s and 1960s, the institutional unitary and professional identity of the NEA began to erode, and its role as "spokesorganization" on national problems in education changed dramatically. As a result, we note that the commissions in the post-World War II era were most often underwritten by private foundations, and *A Nation at Risk* was government initiated.

Who Served on the Commissions Directing the Studies?

Our findings concerning the actors selected to produce the reports confirm Tyack's ideas about an administrative elite who dominate reform discussions.[50] The most typical commission member prior to 1960 was the educational administrator, whether from the college, district, or school; few if any of the "experts" were women, teachers, or representatives of minority groups. The more recent commissions maintained these characteristics, though more women and minorities were represented on them. Silberman has suggested that it is because university administrators and professors produce reform reports that their recommendations are doomed to fail.[51] In addition, most of the commissions had a strong chairman (all were male), who dominated and guided the study and report preparation and who, in many cases, had formulated a position on school reform prior to their heading up a commission.

How Were the Studies Conducted?

The most striking feature in our analysis of how the studies were conducted is their unscientific nature. Except for the Progressive Education Association's *Eight Year Study*, Conant's *The American High School Today*, and Boyer's *High School*, no semblance of scientific inquiry attended the collection of data or preparation of final reports. Most of the commissions relied on consultants for advice before preparing conclusions. Even the three more analytic studies did not carefully follow the accepted canons of social science research. Virtually all the findings and recommendations presented in the reports, then, are potentially skewed to reflect the biases of the panels of experts or chairmen who wrote them. And, in the end, it is the reputation of the experts and sponsoring organizations, more than the rigor of their methodologies, that lends legitimacy to commission reports.

Which Aspects of Schooling Were Given the Most Attention in the Reports?

Given our goals here, the reports we analyzed focused on high school curricula. Most of them called for some form of core curriculum for all students, but allowed for choices that could respond to the diversity of students attending American high schools. A second most frequent focus was the functions or purposes of the high school. Here we see each report as a mirror of its age. The Committee of Ten report, written when most high schools were college preparatory, held a strongly academic orientation; the thrust of the efficiency era was apparent in the *Cardinal Principles*'s call for schools to help create a social order; the reports of the PEA reflected progressive thinking on alternative curricula and students' needs; the Conant report emphasized the academically gifted at a time when Sputnik challenged our ability to compete with Soviet gains in science and technology; the Kettering report, following the 1960s, identified the egalitarian functions of the school during a period when civil and individual rights shaped the public consciousness; and the reports of the 1980s discuss quality (at a time when schools are generally under attack) and comparative international education (at a time when our national ability to compete economically is being challenged). The predominant policy goals of this century—efficiency, equity, and quality—are clearly reflected in the concerns of the commissions and the reports they issued.

What Were the Principal Findings and Recommendations in the Reports?

The reports all present a wide array of findings and recommendations that cannot be summarized in simple terms. Consistent with their predominant focus discussed above, however, most of the reports outline a prescribed high school curriculum, with a certain degree of latitude for choice built in.

In some ways, it is easier and more instructive to discuss the elements the commissions tended to avoid. For example, the reports do not recommend any structural changes, beyond the consolidation of smaller high schools (Conant), exploration of alternative schools (National Commission on the Reform of Secondary Education), and longer years or days of study (*Education for ALL Youth, Making the Grade*, and *A Nation at Risk*). Michael Katz's metaphor is appropriate here—a box whose contents are continually reshuffled, while the box itself remains intact.[52] Given the problems that all the reports identified in their findings, the tacit acceptance of "the one best system" is surprisingly strong.

Another characteristic of the reports' recommendations is their lack of specificity. With very few exceptions, the reports presented ideal states, whose lack of concreteness make it difficult to know what is meant. For example, several reports called for schools to prepare students for work, some even suggest general courses. Yet most schools throughout the century could reasonably argue they provided these very things. Differences between school practices and commission recommendations, then, would be matters of degree or intent. Even the more formalized recommendations on curricula lack enough specificity to be easily implemented. For example, the NCEE, Conant, and Kettering (National Commission on the Reform of Secondary Schooling) prescriptions for three years of English or "English I, II, and III" sound more explicit than they turn out to be. The substance of such courses is not self-evident, and the idea that all high school students, regardless of their functional literacy or interests, could profit from such courses is problematic.

What Impact Did the Reports Have?

Most scholars who have analyzed reports agree that reform commission recommendations have had little direct impact on schools.

Some writers say that reform reports generated discussion, or they show how schools conformed over time to the general guidelines the reports laid out. Yet the studies we found that attempted to analyze the direct impact of recommendations on schools were consistently negative; it appears that school systems generally do not adopt reform report proposals or put them into practice. Given the unscientific nature of commission inquiries and the lack of specificity in commission recommendations, their limited impact is understandable.

THE TRIUMPH OF REFORM?

When all facets of the reports are analyzed, the endurance of the national commission effort at reform is striking. Panels of notable educators and civic leaders, spanning ninety years, have found short-comings—sometimes with alarm—in the secondary schools of America. In one after another investigation characterized by the collection of data and opinions, the commissions have offered general recommendations for change, without much documented effect upon educational practice.

Given the historical record, one might expect that the forces who were moved to create new panels of expert critics would have learned to be less sanguine in their expectations or to give up on the national commission process altogether. However, one way to understand the commissions' persistence is to observe that until recently commission organizers have had no comprehensive and analytical studies of the commission process to inform them.

Yet, even in the face of the education commission history and its limited impact on schools and classrooms, the commission reform process may endure. Slater and Warren suggest that it may play an indirect part in the cyclical revitalization of public education in the United States.[53] The reform process, aided by the national commission reports, may reinforce periodic movements of institutional self-renewal. And in this regard, "it is essential to the triumph of reform that it shall never succeed."[54]

NOTES

1. National Education Association, *Report of the Committee on Secondary School Studies* (Washington, D.C.: Government Printing Office, 1893), National Commission on Excellence in Education, *A Nation at Risk: The Imperative for Educational Reform* (Washington, D.C.: Government Printing Office, 1983).

2. C. E. Silberman, *Crisis in the Classroom: The Remaking of American Education* (New York: Random House, 1970): J. S. Coleman, T. Hoffer, and S. Kil-

gore, *High School Achievement: Public, Catholic, and Private Schools Compared* (New York: Basic Books, 1982); J. I. Goodlad, *A Place Called School* (New York: McGraw-Hill, 1984); and T. Sizer, *Horace's Compromise: The Dilemma of the American High School* (Boston: Houghton Mifflin, 1984).

3. National Education Association, *Report of the Committee on Secondary School Studies*.

4. H. J. Perkinson, *The Imperfect Panacea: American Faith in Education, 1865-1965* (New York: Random House, 1968), p. 134.

5. See, for example, T. Sizer, *Secondary Schools at the Turn of the Century* (New Haven: Yale University Press, 1964), pp. 183-99.

6. L. A. Cremin, *The Transformation of the School* (New York: Alfred A. Knopf, 1964).

7. Perkinson, *The Imperfect Panacea*, p. 136.

8. E. P. Cubberley, *Public Education in the United States* (Boston: Houghton Mifflin, 1934), p. 543.

9. E. G. Dexter, "Ten Years' Influence of the Report of the Committee of Ten," *School Review* 14 (April 1906): 269.

10. Perkinson, *The Imperfect Panacea*, p. 137.

11. E. A. Krug, *The Shaping of the American High School, 1880-1920*, vol. 1 (New York: Harper & Row, 1964), p. 295.

12. Commission on the Reorganization of Secondary Education, *The Cardinal Principles of Secondary Education*, Bulletin No. 35 (Washington, D.C.: Government Printing Office, 1918).

13. R. E. Callahan, *Education and the Cult of Efficiency* (Chicago: University of Chicago Press, 1962).

14. Krug, *The Shaping of the American High School*, vol. 1, p. 355.

15. Ibid., p. 394.

16. Ibid., p. 389.

17. T. H. Briggs, "The Secondary School Curriculum: Yesterday, Today, and Tomorrow," *Teachers College Record* 52 (April 1951): 408-9.

18. Cremin, *The Transformation of the School*; and R. F. Butts, "The Search for Purpose in American Education," *College Board Review* 65 (1975-76): 76-82.

19. A. H. Passow, *Reforming Schools in the 1980s: A Critical Review of the National Reports* (New York: Teachers College, Columbia University/ERIC Clearinghouse on Urban Education, 1984), p. 14; E. A. Krug, *The Shaping of the American High School, 1920-1941*, vol. 2 (Madison, Wis.: University of Wisconsin Press, 1972), p. 252.

20. Passow, *Reforming Schools in the 1980s.*

21. Krug, *The Shaping of the American High School*, vol. 2, p. 4.

22. Department of Secondary School Principals, "Issues of Secondary Education: Report of the Committee on the Orientation of Secondary Education," *Bulletin of the Department of Secondary School Principals* 20 (January 1936); and Department of Secondary School Principals, "Functions of Secondary Education: Report of the Committee on the Orientation of Secondary Education," *Bulletin of the Department of Secondary School Principals* 21 (January 1937).

23. Krug, *The Shaping of the American High School*, vol. 2, p. 274.

24. Ibid.

25. D. Tyack and E. Hansot, *Managers of Virtue: Public School Leadership in America, 1820-1980* (New York: Basic Books, 1982); Krug, *The Shaping of the American High School*, vol. 2, p. 272.

26. Educational Policy Commission, *The Unique Functions of Education in American Democracy* (Washington, D.C.: National Education Association, 1937); and Educational Policy Commission, *The Purposes of Education in American Democracy* (Washington, D.C.: National Education Association, 1938).

27. Krug, *The Shaping of the American High School*, vol. 2, p. 244.

28. Ibid.

29. Ibid., p. 253.

30. Ibid., p. 256; and Perkinson, *The Imperfect Panacea*, pp. 199-201.

31. W. J. Aiken, *Story of the Eight Year Study* (New York: McGraw-Hill, 1942).

32. F. L. Redefer, "The Eight Year Study—Eight Years Later" (Ph.D. dissertation, Teachers College, Columbia University, 1952).

33. Educational Policy Commission, *Education for ALL American Youth* (Washington, D.C.: National Education Association, 1944); and Educational Policy Commission, *Education for ALL American Youth, A Further Look* (Washington, D.C.: National Education Association, 1952).

34. H. L. Caswell, *The American High School: Its Responsibility and Opportunity* (New York: Harper and Brothers, 1946), p. 258.

35. J. B. Conant, *The American High School Today* (New York: McGraw-Hill, 1959.)

36. Passow, *Reforming Schools in the 1980s*.

37. S. P. Marland, Jr., "Career Education: A Report," in *Conference Report on American Youth in Mid-Seventies* (Washington, D.C.: National Association of Secondary School Principals), cited by Passow in *Reforming Schools in the 1980s*, p. 18.

38. National Commission on the Reform of Secondary Education, *The Reform of Secondary Education: A Report to the Public and the Profession* (New York: McGraw-Hill, 1973.)

39. G. Cawelti, "A Review of the Reports' Advice to the Public and the Profession," *NASSP Bulletin* 58 (1974), p. 93.

40. W. Van Til, "Reform of the High School in the Mid-1970s," *Phi Delta Kappan* 56 (1975): 493-94.

41. Mortimer J. Adler, *The Paideia Proposal* (New York: Macmillan, 1982.)

42. W. D. Hawley, "*The Paideia Proposal*: Noble Ambitions, False Leads, and Symbolic Politics," *Education Week* 2, 12 (24 November 1982).

43. Twentieth Century Fund Task Force on Federal Elementary and Secondary Education Policy, *Making the Grade* (New York: Twentieth Century Fund, 1983).

44. W. Feinberg, "Fixing the Schools: The Ideological Turn," *Issues in Education* 3 (Fall 1985): 113-38.

45. E. L. Boyer, *High School: A Report on Secondary Education in America* (New York: Harper & Row, 1983).

46. Coleman et al., *High School Achievement*; and Goodlad, *A Place Called School*.

47. D. Ravitch, "Curriculum in Crisis: Connections between Past and Present," in *Challenge to American Schools: The Case for Standards and Values*, ed. J. H. Bunzel (New York: Oxford University Press, 1985), pp. 63-78.

48. "Symposium on the Year of the Reports: Responses from the Educational Community," *Harvard Educational Review* 54 (February 1984); "After the Great Debate," *Phi Delta Kappan* 66 (April 1984); and "The National Reform Reports," *Education and Urban Society* 17 (February 1985).

49. R. K. Wimpelberg and R. Ginsberg, "Are School Districts Responding to *A Nation at Risk*?" *Education and Urban Society* 17 (February 1985): 186-203.

50. D. B. Tyack, *The One Best System: A History of American Urban Education* (Cambridge, Mass.: Harvard University Press, 1974).

51. Silberman, *Crisis in the Classroom*, p. 179.

52. M. B. Katz, *Class, Bureaucracy, and Schools: The Illusion of Educational Change in America* (New York: Praeger, 1975).

53. R. O. Slater and D. R. Warren, "The Triumph of School Reform," *Education and Urban Society* 17 (February 1985): 119-25.

54. W. Hazlitt, quoted in Slater and Warren, "The Triumph of Reform."

BIBLIOGRAPHY

Adler, Mortimer J. *Paideia Proposal*. New York: Macmillan, 1982.

"After the Great Debate." *Phi Delta Kappan* (April 1984).

Aiken, W. J. *Story of the Eight Year Study*. New York: McGraw-Hill, 1942.

Boyer, E. L. *High School: Report on Secondary Education in America*. New York: Harper & Row, 1983.

Briggs, T. H. "The Secondary School Curriculum: Yesterday, Today, and Tomorrow." *Teachers College Record* 52 (April 1951): 399-448.

Butts, R. F. "The Search for Purpose in American Education." *College Board Review* 65 (Winter 1975/76): 76-82.

Callahan, R. E. *Education and the Cult of Efficiency*. Chicago: University of Chicago Press, 1962.

Caswell, H. L. *The American High School: Its Responsibility and Opportunity*. New York: Harper and Brothers, 1946.

Cawelti, G. "A Review of the Reports' Advice to the Public and the Profession." *NASSP Bulletin* 58 (1974): 86-93.

Coleman, J. S.; Hoffer, T.; and Kilgore, S. *High School Achievement: Public, Catholic, and Private Schools Compared*. New York: Basic Books, 1982.

Commission on the Reorganization of Secondary Education. *The Cardinal Principles of Secondary Education*, Bulletin No. 35. Washington, D.C.: Government Printing Office, 1918.

Commission on the Reorientation of Secondary Education. *Issues of Secondary Education*. Washington, D.C.: National Education Association, 1936.

_____. *Functions of Secondary Education*. Washington, D.C.: National Education Association, 1936.

Conant, J. B. *The American High School Today*. New York: McGraw-Hill, 1959.

Cremin, L. A. *The Transformation of the School*. New York: Alfred A. Knopf, 1964.

Cubberley, E. P. *Public Education in the United States*. Boston: Houghton Mifflin, 1934.

Department of Secondary School Principals. "Issues of Secondary Education: Report of the Committee on the Orientation of Secondary Education." *Bulletin of the Department of Secondary School Principals* 20 (January 1936).

_____. "Functions of Secondary Education: Report of the Committee on the Orientation of Secondary Education." *Bulletin of the Department of Secondary School Principals* 21 (January 1937).

Dexter, E. G. "Ten Years' Influence of the Report of the Committee of Ten." *School Review* 14 (April 1906).

Educational Policy Commission. *The Unique Functions of Education in American Democracy*. Washington, D.C.: National Education Association, 1937.

_____. *The Purposes of Education in American Democracy*. Washington, D.C.: National Education Association, 1938.

_____. *Education for ALL American Youth*. Washington, D.C.: National Education Association, 1944.

_____. *Education for ALL American Youth, A Further Look*. Washington, D.C.: National Education Association, 1952.

Feinberg, W. "Fixing the Schools: The Ideological Turn." *Issues in Education* 3 (Fall 1985): 113-38.

Goodlad, J. I. *A Place Called School*. New York: McGraw-Hill, 1984.

Hawley, W. D. *"The Paideia Proposal*: Noble Ambitions, False Leads, and Symbolic Politics." *Education Week* 2, 12, 24 November 1982.

Katz, M. B. *Class, Bureaucracy, and Schools: The Illusion of Educational Change in America*. New York: Praeger, 1975.

Krug, E. A. *The Shaping of the American High School, 1880-1920*, vol. 1. New York: Harper & Row, 1964.

_____. *The Shaping of the American High School, 1920-1941*, vol. 2. Madison, Wis.: University of Wisconsin Press, 1972.

Marland, Jr., S. P. "Career Education: A Report." In *Conference Report on American Youth in Mid-Seventies*. Washington, D.C.: National Association of Secondary School Principals.

National Commission on Excellence in Education. *A Nation at Risk: The Imperative for Educational Reform*. Washington, D.C.: Government Printing Office, 1983.

National Commission on the Reform of Secondary Education. *The Reform of Secondary Education: A Report to the Public and the Profession*. New York: McGraw-Hill, 1973.

National Education Association. *Report of the Committee on Secondary School Studies.* Washington, D.C.: Government Printing Office, 1893.

"The National Reform Reports." *Education and Urban Society* 17 (February 1985).

Passow, A. H. *Reforming Schools in the 1980s: A Critical Review of the National Reports.* New York: Teachers College, Columbia University/ERIC Clearinghouse on Urban Education, 1984.

Perkinson, H. J. *The Imperfect Panacea: American Faith in Education, 1865-1965.* New York: Random House, 1968.

Ravitch, D. "Curriculum in Crisis: Connections between Past and Present." In *Challenge to American Schools: The Case for Standards and Values,* edited by J. H. Bunzel, pp. 63-78. New York: Oxford University Press, 1985.

Redefer, F. L. "The Eight Year Study—Eight Years Later." Ph.D. dissertation, Teachers College, Columbia University, 1952.

Silberman, C. E. *Crisis in the Classroom: The Remaking of American Education.* New York: Random House, 1970.

Sizer, T. *Horace's Compromise: The Dilemma of the American High School.* Boston: Houghton Mifflin, 1984.

_____. *Secondary Schools at the Turn of the Century.* New Haven: Yale University Press, 1964.

Slater, R. O., and Warren, D. R. "The Triumph of School Reform." *Education and Urban Society* 17 (February 1985): 119-25.

"Symposium on the Year of the Reports: Responses from the Educational Community." *Harvard Educational Review* 54 (February 1984).

Twentieth Century Fund Task Force on Federal Elementary and Secondary Education Policy. *Making the Grade.* New York: Twentieth Century Fund, 1983.

Tyack, D. B. *The One Best System: A History of American Urban Education.* Cambridge, Mass.: Harvard University Press, 1974.

Tyack, D., and Hansot, E. *Managers of Virtue: Public School Leadership in America, 1820-1980.* New York: Basic Books, 1982.

Van Til, W. "Reform of the High School in the Mid-1970s." *Phi Delta Kappan* 56 (1975): 493-94.

Wimpelberg, R. K., and Ginsberg, R. "Are School Districts Responding to *A Nation at Risk?*" *Education and Urban Society* 17 (February 1985): 186-203.

PART THREE

THEORIES OF COMMUNITY DEVELOPMENT AND PERSONAL ENHANCEMENT

4

Social and Community Development: A Function of Education

Michael K. Grady and Faith A. Sandler

The history of schooling in the United States is a history of innovation and idealism. Public education as a right of citizenship has been a source of constant change in American society. Our schools represent the greatest receptor of hope for social reform and stability, and continue to be the arena in which the struggle for equality is waged.

In examining the intersections of social advancement and education, we have chosen four theoretical bases for the social goals of schools: Americanization; economic and technological advancement; equalization and stratification; and the maintenance of diversity. These categories represent an instructive framework for examining educational reform. We present them somewhat chronologically; however, areas of overlap not only exist but serve to illuminate the fact that the societal goals of education cannot be completely isolated from one another or from the consistent presence of education as a vehicle for individual advancement.

Rarely have we, as a society, completely abandoned a particular social goal of our schools. Historically, we have rearranged, modified, and rediscovered each of the goals we discuss in this chapter. While these four sections are arranged chronologically, theoretical reference points from preceding sections will be used to demonstrate the continuity of particular social goals of schooling.

As a society of diverse citizens engaged in fierce economic competition, we have relied upon the public schools to prepare both wage laborers and great leaders. We have wanted to believe in the ability of education to create a society in which social and economic rewards are truly based upon merit. During several periods of our history, we have worked to translate that belief into educational policy. However, the fact that we have not yet succeeded in creating such a society is not cause for disillusionment. Continued examination of the process of advancing a society through its schools is indeed an essential task for theorists and policymakers alike. The relationship between social structure and teaching and learning can be a determinant in racial and social oppression as well as in liberation and equality. The more we seek to learn about that critical relationship, the better our chances of creating a society that more closely conforms to our ideals.

THE DRIVE TO AMERICANIZE

Public pressure for official action to hasten the assimilation of foreign influences has taken on varying levels of intensity during the course of American history. Closely associated with the concentration of foreign immigrants and society's perception of the socially desta-bilizing influence of these new arrivals, Americanization efforts have paralleled the major waves of immigration to this country. As diverse groups arrived on American soil, schools were vested with the respon-sibility of instilling common cultural and social attributes in these new Americans. The role of the school in immigrant assimilation strategies represented the search for shared and teachable definitions of this country and its democratic ideals.

Demographic Characteristics of the Immigrant Populations

Hutchinson observed this phenomenon of the relationship between immigration and education by examining data derived from decennial population statistics from 1890 to 1950. The foreign-born popula-tion in this country, the category traditionally defined as the immi-grant populace, peaked at 14.7 percent of the total U.S. population in 1890, dropped to 11.6 percent in 1930, and leveled off at slightly less than 7 percent in 1950. Corollary statistics behaved similarly. Native-born of foreign or mixed parentage paralleled immigration figures with a time lag of one generation, or roughly twenty years. Offspring of immigrants constituted 23.5 percent of the American population in 1930. The aggregate statistic that reflects total foreign influence, the foreign stock category, was just less than 40 percent in 1910, slipping to 36.2 percent in 1930, and 25 percent in the decade ending after World War II.

The country-of-origin composition of the foreign born, for both external and internal factors, was widely distributed among sending nations, depending on the period of immigration. Northern and Western Europeans dominated the immigration rolls throughout the nineteenth century. By 1920 this mix had shifted, with much of the immigration coming from Eastern Europe and the Mediterranean countries. Following World War I, immigrants came primarily from the countries of the Western Hemisphere, especially Mexico, Canada, and the island nations of the Caribbean.

Most demographers point to 1920 as the critical date for foreign immigration to the United States (Duncan, 1933). The war produced a heightened sense of national insecurity concerning foreign influence, largely for political reasons. Before the "transatlantic movement could resume . . . the U.S. had embarked on a policy of numerical limitation of migration by country of origin" (Hutchinson, 1956: 268). In effect, immigration officials developed a cultural pecking order of foreign nationals with restrictions placed on peoples from nations that posed a perceived threat to national security or whose citizens had experienced more difficulty adapting to American customs in the past. Immigration was further slowed by a corresponding decrease in traffic from "chosen nations," namely citizens of the British Isles and northern Europe.

Clear patterns of occupational and geographical distribution existed for immigrants and their children during the great age of mass foreign settlement in this country (Higham, 1966). By the 1920s this had become an increasingly urban phenomenon, especially among the Poles, Irish, Russians, and Greeks migrating from the great capitals of Europe. Large cities along the Eastern Seaboard and the Great Lakes contained sprawling ghettos of these European immigrants. On the other hand, Scandinavian and Mexican immigrants tended toward familiar agrarian life-styles, the former often settling in the upper Midwest, the latter in California or the Southwest.

Following World War I, the percentage of immigrants in the labor force peaked at 45 percent (Korman, 1967). A high concentration of the foreign born worked as day laborers, machine operators, service workers, craftsmen, and skilled laborers. Far fewer were active in agriculture and the professions. Hutchinson found that "occupational continuity was intergenerational," with status and income levels rising first for Eastern Europeans, followed by the Greeks, Canadians, and in a less fluid way, the Mexicans. The "foreign stream" slowed to a trickle during the depression years when the economic incentive to immigrate was less compelling. The outbreak of World War II immersed the American public in another round of xenophobia, prompting one observer to predict in the mid-1950s that "the mortality losses of the foreign born over the next decades will continue to be greater than can be counterbalanced by immigration at the present level" (Hutchinson, 1956: 270).

Societal Response to the Immigrant Population

The American response to these varying levels and cultural tones of immigration ranged from intensive efforts to assimilate the foreign born into the American mainstream, to severe rounds of restriction, usually provoked by events beyond America's shores (Carolson and Coburn, 1972). Milton Gordon developed a two-level definition of assimilation to describe the varying rates of cultural integration for different segments of the immigrant population. The first stage, behavioral assimilation or acculturation, required a "fusion in which individuals of differing ethnic backgrounds acquire the basic habits, attitudes, and lifestyles of an embracing national culture." The second dimension, "structural assimilation, [permitted] the entrance of the immigrant into the social cliques, organizations, institutional activities . . . of the receiving society" (Gordon, 1964: 203). Gordon's interpretation, in effect, examines the extent to which the newcomers are integrated into, or remain independent from, the host culture.

During the first decade of the twentieth century, the school had moved to center stage in the national effort to assimilate the immigrant population. "The school would now be seen as an instrument for promoting the interests of the community rather than the individual" (Weiss, 1982: xiii). By 1909, the U.S. Immigration Commission reported, 57.8 percent of public school students in the thirty-seven largest cities were of foreign-born parentage. In New York and Chicago this proportion exceeded two-thirds.

The issue of language proficiency was central to the efforts of assimilationists, who reasoned that "they [non-Anglophones] will never understand the spirit of the country unless they understand the language of the court and press, the pulpit and forum" (Roberts, 1920: 68). Likewise, citizenship training became a high national priority given the perceived "inseparable relation between the health of the city, the kind of education offered in the schools, the character of public officials and the conscientious use of the ballot" (Roberts, 1920: 78).

Incentives linked to economic security, political stability, and socially acceptable deportment provided momentum for the forces behind the Americanization of the foreign-born populace. Atzmon wrote that the "goal of Americanization" was to effectively liberate the foreigner, permitting him to "increase his family's holdings . . . understand the purpose of the Republic, discharge the obligations of good citizenship . . . and [maintain] the moral requisites to make America the predestined moral mediator of mankind" (1958: 223).

By the time World War I began, concern was mounting over the infectious potential of ideas considered radical that had originated in Europe and were being transported to American intellectual circles for eventual application to organized labor. This development hastened progress on both the educational and restrictionist sides of the Americanization debate. This effort was fueled by the finding that "recruitment among radicals was concentrated in the unintelligent, illiterate 20 percent" (Berry, 1921: 101). Thus, "idealists and philanthropists embarked on a first-class crusade of education and inculcation," hoping to convert the foreign masses into "old-line" Americans (Hartmann, 1948: 268).

The Federal Role in the Push to Americanize

The federal government got into the business of Americanization in 1915 with the publication of *The Federal Textbook on Citizenship Training*, which was distributed to accredited schools, labor groups, factories, YMCAs, and church organizations. The Bureau of Education sponsored such efforts as the America First conference in 1917 and the *Americanization Bulletin*, first published in 1918.

By 1913 New Jersey, Massachusetts, and California had enacted state laws providing public funds for the "creation of educational opportunity for adult and minor immigrants in English language and American citizenship instruction" (Atzmon, 1958: 75). In 1918 Massachusetts adopted a resolution that made immigration education an official function of the state department of instruction. A U.S. Commission of Education survey discovered that by 1925 thirty-four states had provisions for adult education, twenty-seven had concentrated such functions at the state level, twenty-four offered financial aid to locales that provided immigration education services, and fourteen offered special teacher training for adult educators.

By 1919, however, the cry for immigration quotas was on the rise. Growing consternation concerning the fact that "across the ocean in Russia a new economic regime had been established that did not find acceptance with goodly majority of American people" created pressure to cap the flow of ideas and people from targeted European nations (Atzmon, 1958: 271). The concept of "hyphenated Americans" had become anathema to many observers of international affairs;

assimilation efforts were intensified to shore up national security. The "anti-Red drive" of 1919-20 faulted citizenship training techniques for overemphasizing "facts of government, [with] too little stress on the development of a spiritual unity with American institutions, background and national life" (Atzmon, 1958: 79-80).

Thus, a crucial tension emerged between proponents of assimilation and those who favored rigid national immigration quotas. The balance of forces was tipped with the fear generated by the European conflict and the political instability in Tsarist Russia. In 1917 President Wilson signed an immigrant literacy bill that was first introduced two decades earlier. In 1921 Warren Harding placed a 350,000-person limit on foreign immigration to the United States. This was tightened to 150,000 three years later. The latter effort introduced the concept of a "national origins quota system" (Carlson and Coburn, 1972: 349).

Following World War II, concern with the assimilation of foreign-born citizens into the American democratic mainstream shifted focus. With limitations on the number and origins of new immigrants in place, American attention turned toward assuring that the citizenry was now loyal to common concepts of American democracy in the face of extending Communist influence. Schools soon came under scrutiny with respect to their ability to stave off nondemocratic forces (Burton, 1953). They were challenged to do more than simply Americanize; they were now required to assure loyalty and defend democracy.

In spite of a growing concern with inequality in education, the need for a redesigned curriculum to fit a rapidly advancing technology, and other pressing educational issues of the day, the power of the schools to indoctrinate the citizenry was recognized. James Bryant Conant remarked on the importance of education in the preservation of democracy, asserting that "success against the spread of communism in no small measure depends upon the successful operation of our own free society" (1961: 34). Success in the United States, according to Conant, would depend on our ability, through education and other means, to unify people of disparate backgrounds and classes in support of democratic ideals. His concern with the increasing social and economic divisions between slum and suburb was based on what he saw as the ensuing difficulty of maintaining a unified society.

While the investigations of the McCarthy era were cause for consternation on college campuses and school districts where administrators attempted to secure signatures on loyalty oaths, the real outcome of the era was to reaffirm American belief in the power of education and the vulnerability of schools (Ravitch, 1983). The importance of education as the mechanism for perpetuating American ideals was firmly ingrained in the minds of social theorists. The period following the McCarthy era saw a continued wave of immigration to this country. However, the extremism of the red scare resulted in a reformulation of the strategy through which schools "Americanized" the population.

In a recent work on national immigration policy, Nathan Glazer distinguishes contemporary immigration patterns from those that peaked prior to World War I. From 1840-1930 the majority of students in American urban classrooms of the Northeast and Midwest were children whose parents for the most part emigrated from the nations of Europe. Foreign immigration receded for two decades following the war, but by the mid-1960s, "the education of the immigrant . . . [was] as controversial as it ever had been, indeed more controversial than it was during the great age of mass immigration that ended in 1924" (Glazer, 1985: 213). He goes on to state that "in 1924 the gates to the U.S. were in effect closed to all but Europeans from the British Isles and Northwestern Europe; in 1965 this preference was lifted and the gates were widened" (Glazer, 1985: 311).

Glazer contends that the events of the 1960s created a contextual setting that influenced the education of the "new immigrants." Education had become more crucial to economic fate due to structural changes in the national economy. Added to this was the effect of the rapid migration of blacks from southern farmlands, the heightened activism by all three federal branches, especially in the area of civil rights, and the loss of confidence in American institutions occasioned by the war in Vietnam and the urban riots of the 1960s. The net effect of these developments was a drastic change in the rules and conditions under which immigrant children were treated in American schools, coinciding with a change in theories on the social functions of schooling.

EDUCATIONAL REFORM IN PURSUIT OF SOCIOECONOMIC AND TECHNOLOGICAL ADVANCEMENT

In the first decades of the twentieth century, Americans were witness to a level of immigration that rivaled the Irish and German diasporas of the 1840s. The more recent wave, however, had a more profound impact on the system of public education. By 1910 the cities most affected by immigration, namely those of the Northeast and Great Lakes regions, had compulsory attendance laws in effect as a result of the desire to Americanize immigration populations through education and a need to control entry into the work force. The result was a high concentration of children of immigrants enrolled in the public school system. Thus, what we find during this period is an educational system that continued to be sustained by the principles of the common school, a conception that was no longer relevant to the needs of children whose backgrounds and aspirations were vastly different from their predecessors.

Social Health, Economic Transition, and Progressive Education

Many elements of society chose to measure the effectiveness of schools using various indicators of social condition, what Bagley referred to as "social health statistics" (1934: 119). Increased frequencies in such areas as crime, communicable diseases, drunkenness, poorhouse enrollment, etc. were linked to the diminished effectiveness of the schools.

The initial desire of educational planners and government officials was to get the school-age populace into schools through the passage of compulsory attendance laws. By 1910 the enforcement of these laws had achieved a rapid subscription of nonenrolled students. Immigrant parents' aspirations, "the economic, the communal and the civic . . . propelled [them] from central and southern Europe toward a growing concern for education" (Smith, 1969: 542). Similarly, "the immigrants' own hopes for their children account for the immense success of the public school system . . . in drawing the mass of working-class children into its embrace" (Smith, 1969: 543). The thrust of this drive to the schools was based on the new arrivals' conviction that the means to economic success was somewhere contained inside the schoolhouse gate.

Thomas asserted that "any society which accepts within its boundaries members of other societies or cultures, and which attempts to put them on a common basis of activity, will itself change radically in the process" (1954: 253). Emerging from this cultural collage of beliefs, languages, and traditions present in the schools was the public demand to "insure a high level of common culture . . . to the end that the collective thinking and collective decisions of the group may be done on the highest plane possible" (Bagley, 1934: 139). Revolutionary changes in the constitution of the older school systems, both in terms of student needs, backgrounds, and aspirations, begot changes in the academic and organizational structures of the schools.

These changes were partially manifest in a reform of the educational system, which was heavily influenced by the "national consensus about progressive reform in both schools and society" (Smith, 1969: 543). Prior to 1890 the emphasis was on rigidly codified areas of knowledge and skill. The realization that the system had grown obsolete gave rise to the progressive education movement of the early 1900s. Though historians differ on the extent to which the two were related, it is clear that the philosophy of John Dewey and the principles of progressive educators shared many of the ideals that fueled the modernization of the American school.

The publication of *Democracy and Education* in 1906 established Dewey as the most influential educational reformer of the day. In the words of Oscar Handlin, it was Dewey's notion of "communal disintegration" that compelled the school "to intervene, to supply the guides to action that the individual could no longer acquire through the slow accretion of experiences" (1959: 18-19). Dewey's work was criticized as demeaning to the immigrant family unit; indeed, he appeared to be proposing an expansion of the school's *in loco parentis* authority to the exclusion of parental and sibling influence. "The function of the schools," Handlin continued, "was to indoctrinate their students with a positive pattern of beliefs that would guide their acts as citizens. . . . Experience could not be counted on to endow men with the cultural equipment for life's decisions. The school would have to do so" (Handlin, 1959: 19).

The preponderant theme of the period was the economic and political pragmatism of the movement to improve the schools. Cohen writes: "The old idea that knowledge is power is extended to imply that it is the key to individual social and economic status" (1970: 13). He adds that "since the nineteenth century, public education has been viewed as an antidote for the diminishing equality of opportunity generally thought to be associated with cities, industrialization, immigration, and hardening class structure" (1970: 13).

Between 1890 and World War I, observers noted the "inextricable relationship between social reform, reform through education, and reform of education" (Cremin, 1962: 85). The reform movement had its roots in the belief that if the schools could reach a large proportion of the school-age population, and do a better job educating those it reached, the large social and economic menaces could be disarmed. Cremin proposed that this idea "had its origin during the quarter century before World War I in an effort to cast the school as a fundamental lever of social and political regeneration" (1962: 88).

At the same time, municipal agencies were waging a war against the slums in larger American cities. Riis noted that "the whole battle with the slum is fought out, in, and around the public school" (Riis, 1902: 410). Cremin added that this "incredible suffering could be alleviated, neither by charity nor revolution, but in the last analysis, education" (1962: 59). So it was that the belief evolved that education was the mechanism through which all social ills could be treated and increasingly diverse segments of the population could be raised to an equal plane. This was consistent with the pervasive American ideal that equal opportunity for economic and social advancement should be extended to all strata of society, and be based on merit rather than one's hereditary social position. The schools became the key means to such an opportunity.

By the century's turn, the teachers and administrators of America's public schools found themselves in the untenable position of following an instructional program that was ill-equipped to deal with the challenges of the growing ethnic and academic diversity of the public schools. Cubberly's strict interpretation of the obligation of schools was "to break up their [immigrant] groups and settlements, to assimilate or amalgamate these people as part of the American race, and to implant in their children the Anglo-Saxon conception of rightness" (1909: 255). It was incumbent upon the school to adapt its organizational and instructional agenda to the needs and aspirations of this new wave of students.

The first signs of economically related school reform appeared in 1892-93 and were centered on the condition of the secondary school. Declaring secondary education no longer relevant to the occupational and career needs of American adolescents, the Committee of Ten declared that the "free public secondary school be properly adapted to the needs of society" (Thomas, 1954: 264). It was "the insatiable demand of the children of immigrants, inadequately trained in the . . . ways and weft of American society, who were at last to be recognized by the work of the Committee." The primacy of the school was reiterated by the committee as it identified that social institution as "the one agency that may be controlled definitely and consciously by our democracy for the purpose of unifying people" (Thomas, 1954: 264). This unfettered faith in the school as the means to both unify and equalize was a common theme of educational reformers of this period and beyond.

Carl Kaestle also recognized the diminishing relevancy of the school under the prevailing population and economic conditions of the times:

"The increasing transiency, poverty, and diversity of urban school children had rendered the school's program largely ineffective and irrelevant" (1972: 225). It was a common response of planners during this period to simultaneously applaud the successful recruitment of school-age children to the school, while bemoaning the common school curriculum, developed decades before and now hopelessly lost in its growing obsolescence. The most visible and immediate impact of this reform movement was the differentiation of the common school curriculum. This development recognized the diversity of needs that were then present in the schools; the aspirations of the new students, particularly those at the secondary level, could no longer be fulfilled solely through the study of Copernicus and the classics.

The initial response of the school to this contextual change was the introduction of manual education as an alternative to academic coursework. Students were thought to possess different innate abilities requiring different training for positions in the work force. Originally conceived as an attempt to teach the value of handiwork, it was later faulted as "the institutional expression in a tracking system based largely on social class origins" (Kaestle, 1972: 227). The notion of the self-fulfilling prophecy, that tendency among counselors and other school personnel to steer students toward either the precollegiate courses or the vocational program, created the first germ of doubt about the fairness of the system of differentiated curriculum.

Similar changes were instituted at the elementary school level during this period. The dutiful application of child development theory to the design of the instructional agenda was introduced at this time and represented the cornerstone of the progressive program. The purpose of this theoretical orientation was to prepare the school for the twentieth-century challenges of student diversity. The teaching of applied sciences such as industrial arts and home economics at the secondary school level was also implemented during this wave of reform, extending the function of the school to areas previously reserved for parents.

Educational reform flourished during the interbellum period, resulting in the restructuring of the American school on several levels. First, curriculum reform introduced the notion of vocational training as an alternative to the classical core courses of the common school; at the high school level this concept evolved into several separate curriculum tracks. Second, the organizational structure of the school followed a more rigid classical design with a top-down flow of authority. Teachers were held accountable for their students' progress and principals were evaluated on the aggregate accomplishments of individual school units. Third, classical approaches to organization, common in industry of the period, were applied to the school. Notions of accountability, evaluation, and cost-effectiveness were widely applied to public schools. Pedagogy, armed with the scientific method, tested the validity of well-worn instructional and evaluation techniques.

Mortimer Smith observed in 1949 that "during the past fifteen years a new political phenomenon [appeared], bureaucrats managed by the expert planner who believes quite sincerely that government power must be vastly enlarged if their efforts . . . are to succeed" (1949: 89). Two years prior, the American Association of School Administrators had published *Schools of a New World* in which they proposed that "unreserved priority must be given to the unity and well-being of our society as a whole [by] a vast stepping up of government on all levels" (Smith, 1949: 91). Smith labeled this movement the "power philosophy," the notion that the stronger the concentration of official power behind an effort to change, the more likely such a change will succeed and then survive subsequent attempts to eliminate it.

Progressivism waned abruptly following World War II. According to Cremin, "[it] collapsed because it failed to keep pace with the continuing transformation of American society. . . . The great migrations were over" (Cremin, 1962: 350-51). The social pressure for amalgamation of the various cultural groups was minimal due to the abrupt decrease in the number of school-age children of foreign parentage. This, together with the advance of the mass media, social welfare agencies, and factory-based instruction "transformed the balance of forces in education" (Cremin, 1962: 350-51). Throughout the first half of the century, the progressives had pushed for an expansion of the school's role in society. The 1950s, due largely to technological advances, required a more refined notion of what the school should provide its constituents.

The Fall of Progressivism and the Launching of Sputnik

The Soviet launching of Sputnik in 1957 is often credited with awakening the American government, and subsequently the schools, to the need for increased academic attention to the sciences and the skills necessary to compete in a technologically advancing world. The push for higher standards in the schools accompanied a general feeling that America had "fallen behind."

The link between the national economy, political power, and education were certainly not "discovered" in the 1950s. Educational theorists and policymakers had been concerned for some time with matching schooling to the needs of burgeoning industry. Big business was rapidly replacing entrepreneurship in the cities, and this, coupled with rapid mechanization, resulted in a definite need for workers with skills different than those of the past (Perkinson, 1977: 97-99). Classical, well-rounded educational programs instituted prior to the wide-scale urbanization of the early twentieth century did not meet the needs of industrialization (Violas, 1978).

While educators had grappled with the question of how to produce laborers to meet market needs, efforts to involve the federal government in setting standards and subsidizing education were largely unsuccessful until the launching of Sputnik (Ravitch, 1983: 229). The National Defense Education Act, signed in 1958, provided federal funds to encourage study and improve instruction in science, math, and foreign languages.

Social scientists and educators began to turn their attention to the critical problem of educating children, in particular ethnic and minority children, in skills completely unknown to the generations before them. The pace of industrial and technological change necessitated "the training of the child in new ways of thought and behavior unlike those learned by the child's parent if the child is to be prepared for adult roles in a changing world" (Eddy, 1967: 18). Schools were now responsible for keeping America equipped with a trained work force and supplying the scientists and engineers necessary to compete with other countries.

Standardized Testing and the Pursuit of Excellence

The precepts of economic success in the United States rely upon the underlying concept of meritocracy. If you are educated, use your intelligence, and work hard, the American ideal holds that you will become successful. While it is not our purpose here to determine the truth of this concept for individuals, it is important to understand that this logic required "objective" measures of intelligence and achievement. If a goal of education is to prepare students for a position in the American economic structure, and if this nation is to compete with others technologically, then it is considered essential that educators be able to measure and to determine the best candidates for various positions in the economic and occupational structure (Hurn, 1978: 125-27).

Standardized testing grew out of the need to group students according to ability and identify "the able, the normal, and the slow from the start, to provide them with appropriate instruction, and by secondary school to sort them out according to their likely careers" (Tyack, 1973: 203-4). The belief in equal educational opportunity was all well and good, but no delay could be sustained in determining the individuals best suited to provide necessary leadership in the science and technology fields. Likewise, the standardized testing movement provided educators with what they believed were predictors of the possible occupational and/or economic positions of individuals based on innate ability.

Debates over the use of standardized tests continue today. While they are heavily used as indicators of intelligence and achievement, they have inspired debate in scholarly and public arenas for their subjectivity, ethnic, class and racial bias, and the concern that intelligence is not so easily measured as the proponents of the I.Q. test would indicate (Kagan, 1975). The effects of continued use of the I.Q. test are detrimental to students of minority or ethnic groups, according to Knowles and Prewitt (1969: 37):

> In spite of the evidence indicating that present I.Q. tests are economically, racially, and culturally biased, I.Q. scores are usually the basis for a child's placement into an ability group. The test results strongly influence the teacher's attitude toward the student. Consequently, a student's scores largely determine the quality of education he will receive, an education which in turn continues to affect his test performance.

Thus, while standardized tests were developed with the goal of more easily fitting schools and students to the needs of the American economy, they have come to represent continued social and economic stratification, which is at odds with the ideals of equality of educational opportunity. Thus, the schools again have moved to center stage as American society attempts to draft them in yet another effort to address systemic ills, this time the problems of poverty, inequality, and the diminishing influence of the family.

EDUCATION AND THE SOCIAL ORDER: EQUALIZATION AND STRATIFICATION

The attempt to formulate educational programs for the public schools that addressed the needs of society at large and served to prepare individuals for their place in life characterized the progressive education movement. As public schools became accessible to larger sectors of the population, and following compulsory attendance legislation, questions of equal educational opportunity and the quality of education provided to minority students came to the forefront.

The School as Equalizer in the Face of Social Change

A source of profound strength lies in the American educational heritage ... designed especially for their task, public schools have stood—and now stand—as great wellsprings of freedom, equality, and self-government.

Educational Policy Commission,
"Public Education and the Future of America," 1955.

This statement of the American Association of School Administrators (AASA) came at a time when the school as a social institution was approaching another transformation point, change brought on by a combination of social turmoil and changes in the character of the American family. By the late 1960s, these developments engendered bitter debate over what role the public school should play in improving the security and quality of life of the population. The AASA statement appears all the more peculiar in the light of its release at a time when the concept of educational equality was undergoing intense scrutiny by many sectors of American society.

The equality debate received national attention in 1900 with the publication of a *New York Times* survey of the educational resource levels of the nation's school districts. Apparent from the findings of the survey was the striking disparity in funding along racial and regional lines. At the conclusion of its report, the *Times* issued a call for action: "Our democracy is at stake. Good schools are necessary if we want our democratic way of life to flourish" (Fine, 1947: xi).

The American Federation of Labor continued the momentum established by the *Times* survey, "adopting a resolution advocating adequate public schools as the indispensable foundation of a successful democratic society" (Fine, 1947: 216). The National Education Association states that only by shrinking the resource gap between rich and poor districts can we "be confident that the battle fought by Horace Mann one hundred years ago to establish free public education for all will not be fought over again" (Fine, 1947: 221).

But it was the 1954 Supreme Court decision in *Brown* vs. *Board of Education* that forced the issue of equal opportunity to the top of the national agenda. *Brown*, if not inspiring immediate legal precedent, served to jolt the American conscience to contemplate the issue of the unfairness of a system that separated black and white students, the former assigned to educational settings that were perniciously inferior in every respect. The debate widened to embrace other issues of inequality, including the difference in resource levels that existed between city, suburban, and rural districts, as well as those separating the vastly underfinanced South from the rest of the nation.

Beyond achieving equality, another dimension was added to the changing role of the postwar school, Cremin has characterized it as "more direct and fundamental intervention in the education of more and more Americans" (1976: 124). Cremin explored how the most basic institution of American life, the family unit, had been altered in recent years. He identified profound changes associated with modernization. The average size of American households decreased from 4.48 in 1890 to 3.40 in 1930 to 3.0 in 1970" (1977: 98-99). In addition, an alarmingly higher rate of single parent families occurred, as well as an increased proportion of women in the workplace during and after World War II (26 percent in 1948; 51 percent in 1974). This period also witnessed a stronger holding power of schools—74 percent of the school-age population in 1910, 87 percent in 1970. The result of these fundamental changes in American society placed, "at the very least, an added burden on extant institutions, with the result that statements of educational purpose tend significantly to broaden" (Cremin, 1962: 94).

Black Americans and the Right to Equal Education

Changing social conditions in the 1950s and 1960s coincided with growing demands from black Americans for access to the democratic process. Their insistence upon equal opportunity, the right to vote, and their belief that education was necessary for economic advancement combined to cause a prolonged confrontation between black Americans and what they perceived to be an inconsistency between American democratic principles and official action.

The tendency in the southern United States to educate black students in separate schools and to provide an educational program tailored to the place in southern society accorded to blacks (agricultural labor, domestic service, semiskilled labor, etc.) was challenged both by leaders of the black community and northern white liberals. An important factor in the process of challenging the law and the acceptable standards regarding the education of blacks in this country was the dispersal of the black population. The period from the mid-1930s to the *Brown* decision included several major changes in the economic and social order of the country.

The migration of southern blacks to northern cities was a process that gained momentum as a result of the Dust Bowl, the aftermath of the Great Depression, and the requirements of wartime industries. The twenty years prior to the *Brown* decision saw increasing industrialization, escalating competition between blacks and whites for limited employment, and a weakening of the ability of American educators to justify separate and patently unequal educational opportunities for black students. The National Association for the Advancement of Colored People began the process of formally challenging discriminatory educational policy in its successful campaign in the 1930s to provide equal salaries for black teachers (Ogbu, 1978: 117).

Gunnar Myrdal described the conflicts inherent in unequal educational opportunities within the American democracy in his classic study of the position of blacks in the United States. Education was considered to be the mechanism whereby both individuals and the society in general could be improved. He characterized American thinkers in this era as "pioneering radical interventionists of the world bent upon improving the human material by means of proper schooling" (Myrdal, 1944: 211). At complete counter-purposes were policies discriminating against blacks in the provision of the basic education necessary to improve the human material and better one's lot in life. This was perhaps the quintessential test case for the American ideal of success and status through individual merit and ceaseless effort. A significant portion of the citizenry, now spread throughout the country, was denied the opportunity to advance as individuals because of racist restrictions imposed upon them as a group.

Several authors have stressed the need, when discussing the early social and legal challenges to racial discrimination in education, to credit the continuous efforts of black thinkers and community leaders to demand recognition of the inequalities of black American life (Knowles and Prewitt, eds., 1969; Ogbu, 1978; Katznelson, 1985). Certainly the growing discomfort among white liberals regarding racial discrimination in education was not born out of isolated intellectual considerations of the democratic ideals. The combined factors of the need for educated labor, the increasingly powerful demands from black citizens, and the widespread realization of the conflict between democratic ideals and current educational policy resulted in the partnership between blacks who demanded that the government and society address their rights and whites who could no longer look the other way. Diane Ravitch contends that the strength of the civil rights movement was the uniqueness of this partnership between popular power and the courts (1983: 138-41). Education as a basic *right* was firmly established by the *Brown* decision. The function of schools to equalize the population so that the democratic ideals of individual merit held ground were reaffirmed by the attempts to provide equal education to black students. Definitions and implementation of the provision of rights to equal education almost immediately became an issue. As a society, we have yet to resolve this issue.

Cultural Deprivation Theories and Compensatory Education

The determination that equal education was a right of all American citizens in *Brown I*, and the decision that school desegregation was to be implemented under the jurisdiction of local schools with district court supervision in *Brown II*, did not end the debate regarding the extent to which schools should function to minimize differences among sectors of American society. Schools were soon expected to make up for supposed deficits created by both the supposed inadequate homes and communities of students exposed to the history of segregation and inequality.

Cultural deprivation theories, always with us, ran rampant in the period following the order of the courts to desegregate public schools. These theories, in sum, held that students not raised in white, middle-class nuclear families were somehow not properly prepared for schooling. Aspects of culture, race, and class became entangled in this attempt to explain lesser levels of achievement among black and Hispanic students. The function of the school in social and community advancement was to "make up" for the disadvantages of coming from a culturally deprived home or community (Bloom, Davis, and Hess, 1965). The social consciousness of the 1960s and 1970s soon transformed this strategy of "blaming the victim" for the mismatch between school and home into an ongoing discussion of the extent to which schools should serve to acculturate students (Reissman, 1962). Kenneth Clark described those who held that cultural deprivation was the cause of unequal education gains as "members of the privileged group who inevitably associate their privileged status with their own innate intellect and its related educational success" (1965: 131).

Scholars and social thinkers engaged in efforts to describe the achievement gaps of ethnic groups or racial minorities by way of the relative distance between the dominant white, Anglo culture of the public school and the differing cultures of the American "melting pot" (Eddy, 1967; Gouldner, 1978). Appropriate education in the ways of the dominant culture, it was believed, was necessary to facilitate academic achievement among racial and ethnic minorities.

Additionally, the question of the extent to which the American school has been affected by the simultaneous drive for equality and the increased role of the school in providing support for more ethnically and economically diverse students has arisen. The school is now faced with the prospect of functioning "in the interest of equalizing opportunity and encouraging individual development, and at the same time achieving a certain measure of socialization for public ends" (Cremin, 1977: 124). In effect, this is similar to the situation of the turn of the century when the schools faced the need to integrate disparate cultures and belief systems into a homogeneous, loyal, and productive populace. The challenges of the 1960s and 1970s were equally formidable.

Attention to economic class and the War on Poverty of the 1960s resulted in concerns about the effect that class has on school success. Critics questioned prevailing theories which held that educational programs that compensated for cultural differences resulted in equal educational opportunity by pointing to economic disparities between groups and the absolute detriments of poverty (Valentine, 1968; Bane and Jencks, 1975; Ogbu, 1978). The American belief in education as an equalizer was challenged on the basis of an examination of the American class structure. Bowles and Gintis led this critique of the functions of schooling in the United States with the assertion that educational reform without economic reform simply serves to perpetuate the existing social order (Bowles and Gintis, 1976).

The principal domestic focus of the nation for the decade and a half that began in 1960 was a volatile compound of race and urban poverty. Amidst the turmoil that resulted from the debate on how to treat the problem, and in particular, the proper role for the educational system, were commentators such as Michael Katz, who were troubled by the increasing number of Americans being held hostage to "a culture of poverty." Galbraith's "case poverty" which was "immune to progress," embraced a growing number of Americans, many black, the majority residing in the sprawling ghettos of the large urban areas.

The deep concern among economists and other students of the problem was the chronic drift of this form of poverty due to changes in economic conditions: "The skill level of the economy is changing and educational deficiency, if anything, becomes an even greater burden. . . . America will have the most literate poor the world has ever known" (Harrington, 1962: 166). Harrington and others beseeched the federal government to bypass the schools in favor of more direct intervention, engaging in a "war on poverty" to wrench victims from the cyclical nature of the problem.

In his epilogue to *Class, Bureaucracy, and the Schools*, Michael Katz reasoned that "schools failed to serve the poor or to reform society in the ways in which their sponsors predicted. Schools did not alleviate poverty and crime, significantly alter social structure, or make society noticeably more democratic" (Katz, 1975: 149).

This bitter indictment of one of America's most cherished institutions ignited a controversy among social scientists over the power of the schools to institute broad social change. One group popularly referred to as the revisionists, asserted that, "by 1965 the schools had polarized American society into self-satisfied whites and victimized blacks, into dependent city dwellers and indifferent suburbanites" (Perkinson, 1977: 220). Some members of this group advanced one step beyond this by claiming that "individuals were shaped [by schools] to serve the national purpose" and "the real purpose of schools was to hold the [oppressed] down" (Perkinson, 1977: 232).

Perkinson's chronicle of revisionism characterizes the movement as surging forward in three separate waves, each extending the reach of the revolutionary platform for educational reform (1977: 235). Wave I, championed by reformers such as Kozol, Kohl, Postman, and Weingartner, proposed serious curriculum reforms in the schools, including modification of traditional teaching methods and the classroom structure. Dennison, Rossman, and Graubard advocated more substantial measures of educational change, what might aptly be classified as radical or structural reform. True reform, argued this group, could only follow the abolition of the current system of schooling and reestablish "free schools"—free, that is, from the inherent constraints imposed to sustain the status quo. Finally, the third wave and death knell of the revisionists, included among its numbers John Holt, Ivan Illich, and Everett Reimer. These individuals proposed the "deschooling" of society, what commentators have since coined as "educational nihilism." It was the panic provoked by the revolutionary proposition that we terminate the American school that scored an abrupt shift in momentum away from the revisionists to the emerging school of thinkers known as "humanistic educators," the founding members being Maslow, Rogers, and Neil.

In her conclusion to *The Great School Wars*, Diane Ravitch identified the central theme of past struggles involving schools: the issue of governance. Whether it be the religious controversies of the mid-nineteenth century, the debate over the influence of the educational expert in the early 1900s, the more recent struggles over race and ethnicity and "community control" of the schools, or the power of the federal bench as exhibited in cases of court-ordered desegregation, the consistent strain throughout this dynamic history of American education is institutional control. Ravitch concludes that "because of the American conception of control of public education, the school is likely to remain at the center of social conflict . . . the underlying contest will continue to reflect fundamental value clashes among discordant ethnic, cultural, racial, and religious groups" (1974: 404). Despite the imminent presence of turmoil around the school as a social institution, Ravitch concludes that "whatever their failings, whatever their accomplishments, the public schools have been and will inescapably be involved in the American search for a viable definition of community" (1974: 404).

The Variables of the Function of Education in the Social Position of Ethnic Groups and Minorities

In the wake of theories regarding the function of the school in maintaining social order, several scholars have provided examinations of the possible variables in the relationship between ethnic groups, education, and social status. Crucial questions exist as to why some ethnic or immigrant groups have succeeded in school, on the whole, while others have not fared so well. These questions reflect an overall question regarding rates and patterns of assimilation for the multitude of people constituting the American citizenry. Education plays an important role in both popular and academic understandings of the process through which a group betters its position in the American social order.

In his classic treatise on patterns of assimilation in the United States, Milton Gordon identified several variables in the process of group assimilation: "The stratifications based on ethnicity are intersected at right angles by the stratifications based on social class, and the social units or blocks of bounded social space created by their intersection are contained in an urban or a rural setting in a particular region of the country" (1964: 47).

With the consideration of education as the primary mechanism for assuring group status enhancement, the question of why some groups have succeeded while others have not has lately been of vital importance to educational and social theorists.

Scholars have considered a critical factor in the ability of a group to use education as a means toward assimilation and advancement in American society to be the relative proximity of the group to the dominant, Anglo-Saxon culture (Handlin, 1957; Gordon, 1964). Among European immigrants, those who came from Mediterranean or Eastern European cultures were less acceptable to the dominant Anglo-Saxon and Germanic culture.

Variables of language and religion are also considered in the rate of ethnic assimilation. The ability of public schools to serve the purpose of equalizing individuals relied upon the existence of a common language. The determination of the individuals involved in framing the terms of American democracy to provide freedom from religious discrimination necessitated the separation of religion from public schooling. The function of the schools in assimilating members of various cultures was differentially successful depending upon the willingness of a given immigrant group to set aside, temporarily or permanently, the language of the homeland and cultural traits related to religion (Bresnick et al., 1978; Crispino, 1980).

Race is the most constraining variable in the social assimilation process, and one that education has only partially addressed. Scholars have attached different degrees of importance to race as a significant factor in educational achievement and assimilation. Ravitch contends that American cities were unable to assimilate black migrants from the South as they had previously assimilated Europeans because the economic conditions in those cities were fundamentally different (1983: 150-53). Early immigrant children who were unsuccessful in school were able to find a place in the work force that, early in the twentieth century, was in need of unskilled or semiskilled labor. Before compulsory attendance laws and the widespread expectation of high school graduation for prospective employees, immigrants did not require public education as a means of assimilation. Blacks who migrated to urban areas of the United States in the period following the depression did so under very different economic conditions than those that existed during earlier waves of European immigration. In addition to the important factors of racism and discrimination, compulsory school attendance and competition for limited jobs did not facilitate assimilation.

Charles Willie includes historical and economic conditions in his analysis of factors affecting the rate of assimilation of ethnics. However, his discussion of the differing levels of group assimilation centers on the dynamic relationship between dominant and subdominant groups. Occupational skills and religious differences must be considered, but the status of blacks in the United States is both an indication of racial discrimination and a result of the response of the black community to that discrimination. Willie contends that the slower rate of assimilation of blacks into the dominant group can be attributed in part to the fact that leaders in the black community have chosen to stay in the community rather than assimilate. While not discounting the affects of racism, Willie asserts that subdominant groups should not be considered powerless in the process of determining their own fate (Willie, 1983).

John Ogbu develops an analysis of the different rates of assimilation for ethnic and minority groups in the United States based on a complex of social and economic factors. He asserts that blacks in the United States can be likened to a caste, and that education and economic opportunity have combined to relegate blacks to the lowest caste status. His analysis is based on the premise that "racial stratification, as distinct from class stratification, generates and sustains patterns of school performance compatible with the educational requirements of the social and occupational roles permitted to the component racial groups and the mode of social mobility characteristic of the system" (Ogbu, 1978: 8).

THE MAINTENANCE OF DIVERSITY AS A FUNCTION OF SCHOOLING

Theories of cultural deprivation as an explanation for the discrepant academic achievement levels of ethnic groups and minorities were succeeded by theories of cultural pluralism and the popular movement to make schools "relevant" to students of differing cultures. Theories of education as a means of assimilation or the arena for the enactment of the "melting pot" gave way to the desire to reaffirm cultural diversity through schooling. Blacks and Hispanics, partially in response to compensatory education movements, began to demand that educational systems not only understand that their children are different but that they celebrate that fact in their policies and curriculum. Additionally, the "new white ethnics" countered by asserting the importance of ethnic background and relevance to all peoples (Stein and Hill, 1977). Schools were expected to serve the purpose of providing culturally relevant instruction as well as reaffirming ethnicity.

Cultural Pluralism

Theories regarding the relationship between education and ethnicity have been characterized by three major types: Anglo-conformity, "melting pot," and cultural pluralism (Gordon, 1964; Crispino, 1980; Bullivant, 1981). Concepts of cultural pluralism refute the notion that assimilation into the predominant Anglo culture is desirable, and are concerned with the idea of the school as the agent of the "melting pot" is a disservice to a nation as ethnically diverse as this one (Pratte, 1979). Cultural pluralists contend that the school serves both society and its students best by not only understanding but by asserting ethnicity.

While the initial educational pluralists were responding to what they considered to be the ethnocentric policies of cultural deprivation and compensatory education, the trend toward asserting one's ethnicity and right to relevant education extended beyond oppressed minorities and recent immigrants (Krickus, 1976; Glazer, 1981). As white ethnics who were third- or fourth-generation immigrants began to "rediscover" their heritage, education became the arena for the competition over *whose* ethnicity would be asserted. "While the white ethnics accuse past American education of trying to erase ethnic awareness, ethnic studies stands ready to homogenize and de-Americanize ethnicity in the name of enhancing difference. Pluralistic education does not so much recognize difference as create and institutionalize it" (Stein and Hill, 1977: 273).

In determining that ethnic minorities and recent immigrants were not to be blamed for failure to succeed in schools that were drastically different, culturally, from their homes and neighborhoods, educational theorists began the struggle over the extent to which educating students toward success in the mainstream is the goal of the school. The variations of ways in which schools were found guilty of misunderstanding students from non-Anglo cultures included the administration and use of I.Q. tests, ability grouping in the classroom, and the more subtle aspects of teacher attitudes (Knowles and Prewitt, 1969: 36-44). Central to the issue of cultural pluralism in education is the question of the responsibility of the schools to prepare students, regardless of background, for entry into a society where the apportionment of power, employment opportunities, and language usage are not determined by theorists but by a dominant power structure. One arena in which these questions have been considered and continue to be of concern is in bilingual education.

Bilingual Education

The end of the nineteenth century in the United States saw the rise of English as the only legitimate public language. While official policy did not dictate the use of the English language, it became the only permissable language for instruction and curriculum in the public schools. With the onset of World War I, Americans began to display a true sense of intolerance toward speakers of foreign languages. The use of languages other than English in public was banned in fifteen states (Krickus, 1976). While some voluntary organizations across the country operated in other languages, English was expected in public settings.

With the signing of the National Defense Education Act in 1958, a slight transition in public opinion of foreign-language usage was evident. Although English was still the only recognized language of the nation, the federal government was offering funds for the teaching and learning of foreign languages. The effect of the insularity of the war years on the capacity of Americans to operate in international circles was of grave concern to the government. While the acquisition of foreign languages was valued, it was framed in terms of national defense and not cultural diversity.

The Bilingual Education Act (Title VII of the Elementary and Secondary Education Act), signed in 1968 by President Johnson, signaled the start of a new and confused era in bilingual/bicultural educational policies in the United States (Ortega, 1973; Thernstrom, 1981). Finding that the exclusive use of English in schools serving non-English-speaking communities denied the right to equal education, the federal government provided funds for instruction in languages other than English (Bullivant, 1981: 120). The signing of the act did not represent wholesale changes in local school policy, however, since representation by local educational authorities was required for a community to petition for funds.

The 1974 Supreme Court ruling in *Lau* vs *Nichols*, however, interpreted the 1964 Civil Rights Act as a specific mandate for state educational policies. The Court ruled that it was the obligation of the public educational system to provide an adequate English base for non-English speakers. Affirmative steps were to be taken to ensure that language did not hamper a student's educational achievement.

For Hispanics in the United States, the bilingual education movement has become a symbol of the struggle for equal educational opportunity and recognition of cultural plurality. "Bilingual education does not necessarily mean education in two languages. It has come to stand for the rights of Hispanics just as busing and integration have stood for the rights of blacks" (Yaffe, 1981: 741). For Hispanics, issues of bilingual education concern not only educational achievement but symbolize ethnic autonomy. Chicano ethnic identity, while obviously not limited to language, is expressed and maintained in Spanish. Hispanic demands for recognition of Spanish by English-speaking educators represent demands for recognition of ethnicity. Policymakers who think that the inclusion of Spanish in the education of Hispanics is enough have misunderstood the demand. Hispanics, in accepting education as the equalizing mechanism of American society, consider the inclusion of Spanish as the key to equal access.

The importance of content, of what schools teach, became apparent in recent decades as blacks, Hispanics, women, and various ethnic groups began to examine and propose revisions in the curriculum of the public schools (Hurn, 1978). A classic liberal arts education including instruction in history that carefully excludes the existence of various ethnic groups and minorities in the past of this country was no longer acceptable. Students, of all backgrounds, were to be educated in the lessons of cultural pluralism and ethnic diversity. If schools are to function in the effort to maintain a pluralistic society, then the content of teaching and learning must reflect human diversity (Hamilton, 1969; Knowles and Prewitt, 1969).

CONCLUSION

Through the first half of the twentieth century, the American system of education had played a key role in the assimilation of millions of immigrants. Though its success rate varied from decade to decade, it cannot be denied that, overall, the school system exhibited a remarkable capacity to provide new arrivals with the linguistic, political, and economic tools needed to function in American society. Between the turn of the century and the end of World War I, people from a mosaic of cultural traditions were brought into the national fold; by the end of World War II, they formed part of a unified national whole.

Postwar optimism with this social and economic stability fostered an attitude of great expectations with regard to the American school. Fresh from the educational accomplishments of the first half of the century, American society began to press its schools once again in the late 1950s and early 1960s. Substantial changes in three key areas of American society necessitated an adjustment in the response of the nation's schools.

The first major development during this period resulted from black Americans' struggle for equal educational opportunity, prompted by the Supreme Court's decision in *Brown* v. *Board of Education*. Though little substantive change occurred in the first decade after the decision, *Brown* would ultimately push the schools to a central position in the national strategy to define and establish equity in education. The re-alignment of attendance zones, student reassignments, and massive compensatory and remedial programs would be developed as a means of relieving decades of separate and unequal schools for this nation's black students. The corresponding pedagogical and organizational impact on the system of education was formidable.

Three years after *Brown*, America awoke to read of the Soviet launching of Sputnik, an event that effectively placed the United States in a position of vulnerability both technologically and, more immediately, in the race for superiority in space. This event was of momentous import to the educational system. America, seemingly pressed to the wall by events outside her borders, again turned to the schools for relief. Public and political pressure precipitated a reorientation of the basic curriculum, with additional emphasis in the areas of math and science. Subsequent changes in the nature of the American economy, specifically the rapid shift in labor demand from manufacturing to service workers, added new dimensions to the school's inherited obligation to train tomorrow's work force.

The War on Poverty of the mid-1960s brought further change in the role of the school in American society. Significant changes in the structure of the American family, with many students being the products of a home environment considered impoverished, required a more active role for the schools in poverty intervention strategies. Massive pieces of legislation were passed during this period, many directed at breaking the vicious poverty cycle through programs directed at the local school level. A far cry from the educational responsibilities of Horace Mann's common school, by the second half of the twentieth century the American schools, especially those in large urban systems, were far more involved in the maintenance of the child's well-being from preschool through graduation. Schools were now obligated to supervise their students' early childhood development, physical and emotional health, special educational needs, and the maintenance of linguistic and cultural traditions of non-English-speaking minorities.

These three structural changes in the American way of life resulted in an abrupt expansion in the scope of responsibility for the American school. Economic, social, and legal requirements have reshaped the role of the school to its current position as the most extensive of any other national system, at any time in history. Tragically, these developments, coupled with the continued invidious effects of racial prejudice, have prevented a replication of early immigrant mobility trends for black and Hispanic Americans. However, it is imperative that when the record of the schools' shortcomings is reviewed, it must be done with a sensitivity to the massive burden we Americans have placed on our system of public education. It is only with an appreciation for such contextual factors that we will reach a true understanding of the level of accomplishment the American system of schooling has achieved as well as be able to modify the system to meet future needs.

REFERENCES

Atzmon, Ezri. 1958. "Educational Programs for Immigrants in the United States." *History of Education Journal* 9, no. 3: 275-80.

Bagley, William C. 1934. *Education and the Emergent Man*. New York: Thomas Nelson & Sons.

Bane, Mary Jo, and Jencks, Christopher. 1975. "The Schools and Equal Opportunity." In *Children of the Cities*, edited by Marvin Leiner, pp. 21-30. New York: Plume Books.

Berry, Charles S. 1921. "Some Problems of Americanization as Seen by an Army Psychologist." *School and Society* 13: 97-104.

Bloom, Benjamin, Davis, Allison, and Hess, Robert. 1965. *Compensatory Education for Cultural Deprivation*. New York: Holt, Rinehart & Winston.

Bowles, Samuel, and Gintis, Herbert. 1976. *Schooling in Capitalist America*. New York: Basic Books.

Bresnick, David, et al., eds. 1978. *Black/White/Green/Red: The Politics of Education in Ethnic America*. New York: Longman.

Bullivant, Brian M. 1981. *The Pluralist Dilemma in Education*. Sydney, Australia: Allen & Unwin.

Burton, William H. 1953. "Education and Social Class in America." *Harvard Educational Review* 22, no. 4.

Carlson, L. H., and Coburn, George A. *In Their Place: White America Defines Her Minorities*. New York: John Wiley & Sons.

Carlton, Frank T. 1908. *Education and Individual Evolution*. New York: Nelson and Sons.

Clark, Kenneth. 1965. *Dark Ghetto: Dilemmas of Social Power*. New York: Harper & Row.

Cohen, David K. 1970. "Immigrants and the Schools." *Review of Educational Research* 40, no. 1: 13-27.

Conant, James Bryant. 1961. *Slums and Suburbs.* New York: McGraw-Hill.

Cremin, Lawrence A. 1962. *The Transformation of the Schools.* New York: Alfred A. Knopf.

———. 1977. *The Traditions of American Education.* New York: Basic Books.

Crispino, James A. 1980. *The Assimilation of Ethnic Groups: The Italian Case.* Staten Island, N.Y.: Center for Migration Studies.

Cubberly, Ellwood P. 1909. *Changing Conceptions of Education.* Boston: Houghton Mifflin.

Duncan, Hannibal G. 1933. *Immigration and Assimilation.* Boston: D. C. Heath.

Eddy, Elizabeth. 1967. *Walk the White Line: Profile of Urban Education.* New York: Anchor Books.

Educational Policy Commission. 1955. *Public Education and the Future of America.* Washington, D.C.: American Association of School Administrators.

Fine, Benjamin. 1947. *Our Children Are Cheated.* New York: Henry Holt & Co.

Glazer, Nathan. 1985. *Clamor at the Gates.* Institute for Contemporary Studies.

———. 1981. "Ethnicity and Education: Some Hard Questions." *Phi Delta Kappan* (January): 386-89.

———. 1979. "Ethnicity in the Schools." In *America and the New Ethnicity*, edited by David Colburn and George Pozzetta. Port Washington, N.Y.: Kennikat Press.

———. 1970. *Beyond the Melting Pot.* With Daniel P. Moynihan. Cambridge, Mass.: The M.I.T. Press.

Gordon, Milton M. 1964. *Assimilation in American Life: The Role of Race, Religion, and National Origins.* New York; Oxford University Press.

Gouldner, Helen. 1978. *Teacher's Pets, Troublemakers and Nobodies: Black Children in Elementary School.* Westport, Conn.: Greenwood Press.

Greer, Colin. 1972. *The Great School Legend.* New York: Basic Books.

Hamilton, Charles V. 1969. "Now That You've Got Your Administration Building Back, What Do You Do Next?" *Chicago Tribune Magazine*, 8 June.

Handlin, Oscar. 1957. *Race and Nationality in American Life.* Boston: Little, Brown & Co.

———. 1959. *John Dewey's Challenge to Education.* New York: Harper Bros.

Harrington, Michael. 1962. *The Other America: Poverty in the United States.* New York: Macmillan.

Hartmann, George E. 1948. *The Movement to Americanize the Immigrant.* New York: AMS Press.

Higham, John. 1966. *Strangers in the Land: Patterns of American Nativism, 1860-1925.* New York: Atheneum.

Hurn, Christopher H. 1978. *The Limits and Possibilities of Schooling.* Boston: Allyn and Bacon.

Hutchinson, E. P. 1956. *Immigrants and Their Children.* New York: John Wiley & Sons.

Kaestle, Carl F. 1972. "Social Reform and the Urban School." *History of Education Quarterly* 12, no. 2: 211-18.

Kagan, Jerome. 1975. "The Enigma of Intelligence." In *Children of the Cities*, edited by Marvin Leiner, pp. 69-80. New York: Plume Books.

Katz, Michael B. 1975. *Class, Bureaucracy, and the Schools*. New York: Praeger.

Katznelson, Ira. 1985. *Schooling for All: Class, Race, and the Decline of the Democratic Ideal*. New York: Basic Books.

_____. "Participation and Political Buffers in Urban America." *Race* 14: 465-80.

Knowles, Louis L., and Prewitt, Kenneth, eds. 1969. *Institutional Racism in America*. Englewood Cliffs, N.J.: Prentice-Hall.

Korman, Gerd. 1967. *Industrialization, Immigrants and Americanizers*. Madison, Wis.: State Historical Society of Wisconsin.

Krickus, Richard. 1976. *Pursuing the American Dream: White Ethnics and the New Populism*. Bloomington, Ind.: Indiana University Press.

Myrdal, Gunnar. 1944. *An American Dilemma: The Negro Problem and Modern Democracy*. New York: Harper Bros.

Ogbu, John. 1978. *Minority Education and Caste: The American System in Cross-Cultural Perspective*. New York: Academic Press.

Ortega, Philip D. 1973. "Chicano Education: Status Quo? Reform? Revolution?" In *Ghosts in the Barrio*, edited by Rafa Poblana, pp. 15-34. San Rafael, Calif.: Leswing.

Perkinson, Henry J. 1977. *The Imperfect Panacea: American Faith in Education, 1865-1976*. 2d ed. New York: Random House.

Pratte, Richard. 1979. *Pluralism in Education*. Springfield, Ill.: Charles C. Thomas.

Ravitch, Diane. 1983. *The Trouble Crusade*. New York: Basic Books.

_____. 1977. *The Revisionists Revised*. New York: Basic Books.

_____. 1974. *The Great School Wars, New York City, 1805-1973. A History of Public Schools as a Battleground of Social Change*. New York: Basic Books.

Reissman, Frank. 1962. *The Culturally Deprived Child*. New York: Harper & Row.

Riis, Jacob A. 1902. *The Battle with the Slum*. New York: Charles Scribner's Sons.

Roberts, Peter. 1920. *The Problem of Americanization*. New York: Macmillan.

Smith, Mortimer B. 1949. *And Madly Teach*. Chicago: Regency.

Smith, Timothy L. 1969. "Immigrant Social Aspirations and American Education." *American Quarterly* 11, no. 3: 523-43.

Stein, Howard F., and Hill, Robert F. 1977. *The Ethnic Imperative: Examining the New White Ethnic Movement*. University Park, Penna: Penn State University Press.

Thernstrom, Abigail. 1981. "Bilingual Miseducation." *New Republic* 184: 15-17.

Thomas, Alan M. 1954. "American Education and the Immigrant." *Teachers College Record* 55 (February): 253-67.

Tyack, David B. 1973. *The One Best System*. Cambridge, Mass.: Harvard University Press.

Valentine, Charles A. 1968. *Culture and Poverty: Critique and Counter-Proposals*. Chicago: University of Chicago Press.

Violas, Paul C. 1978. *The Training of the Urban Working Class*. Chicago: Rand McNally.

Weiss, Bernard J., ed. 1982. *American Education and the European Immigrant*. Urbana, Ill.: University of Illinois Press.

Willie, Charles V. 1983. *Race, Ethnicity, and Socioeconomic Status: A Theoretical Analysis of Their Interrelationship*. Bayside, N.Y.: General Hall, Inc.

Yaffe, Elaine. 1981. "Ambiguous Laws Fuel Debate on Bilingual Education." *Phi Delta Kappan* 62: 740-41.

5

Individual Enhancement as the Personal Purpose of Education

Ann Q. Lynch and Arthur W. Chickering

Belief in the individual as a source of unique potential and in the cultivation of personal talents as a right and a responsibility of the educational system is a basic American tradition. Enhancing the individual has long been a primary goal of education. By providing opportunities for each individual to develop his or her potential, the system contributes to the social good as well as to personal purposes.

OUR AMERICAN CULTURAL HERITAGE

Our American cultural heritage is steeped in the tradition of rugged individualism—from the first explorers of this new continent to the adventurous immigrants. The risk taking and persistence of early settlers seeking religious, political, and economic freedom demonstrated the value of individual initiative and hard work. Pulling one's self up by the bootstraps and making it "come hell or high water" has been a cornerstone of our unique American culture. The land of opportunity awaited the person willing to persevere.

Horatio Alger's success exemplifies that tradition. We have grown up believing that success is possible through personal competence and achievement. Hard work, "stick-to-it-ness," a willingness to delay gratification and to make sacrifices for the long haul, are ingrained American beliefs. Personal competence comes from a natural ability coupled with application and perseverence. Achievement, status, "success" are the just rewards for hard work and sacrifice.

Education, historically the province of the Greek, Roman, English, and European elite, has become the American path to achievement for all citizens, regardless of social class, wealth, or family background.

Franklin's ingenious homilies, the frontier settlers' schoolhouses, and Lincoln's evenings with a slate by the fire are entrenched symbols of American dedication to learning. Child labor laws, compulsory school attendance, land-grant and community colleges and broad-based financial aid all have contributed to that educational ideal. The underlying assumption is that education should help all individuals develop their talents.

Mass public education also has served as the principal means of acculturation for the diverse immigrants coming to this "land of opportunity." Social control and reinforcement of the status quo have occurred as well. Standardized grading, homogeneous classroom grouping, and lecture methods—many of our traditional educational practices—have contributed to uniformity and depersonalization. In many communities, pressures for political, religious, or ethnic conformity have limited individual freedom in learning and teaching.

Counterbalancing the forces for conformity have been the forces for cultural pluralism. Continuing immigration of persons from throughout the world has moved the country from a melting pot to a smorgasbord of needs, interests, and talents. Bilingual classes, ethnic history, and lifelong learning speak to those diverse needs. Our cultural heritage challenges educators to provide opportunities for individual enhancement based on both the traditions of rugged individualism and of cultural pluralism. Most Americans dream of economic, social, and emotional independence. Education can be the key factor in moving persons from conforming, unthinking drones to complex, sensitive, autonomous, and integrated individuals—from a nation of sheep, mass produced by assembly-line practices to a nation of responsible citizens ready to contribute their diverse talents and perspectives to the continued nurturance of our political freedoms and democratic traditions. To do so, we need educational practices that foster individual growth and development while strengthening a sense of interdependence and social responsibility.

BEHAVIORAL SCIENCE PERSPECTIVES

The behavioral sciences provide fundamental perspectives on individual development and enhancement. Sigmund Freud and psychoanalytic thought emphasized individual life experiences. Early childhood events were forces that helped or hindered psychosexual development. Integrating ego, id, and superego and resolving unconscious conflicts became a model for individual development. Alfred Adler focused on conflicts arising from birth order and furthered understanding of power and aggression. His leadership in developing child-guidance clinics contributed to a movement that had significant impact on the individual child. Carl Jung fostered an appreciation of the collective unconscious, characterological archetypes, spiritual development toward wholeness, and dimensions of individual difference according to psychological type.

Several streams of psychological and philosophical thought regarding concepts of the individual gave rise to many of the educational practices of today. The basic assumptions underpinning these practices have to do with belief in the individual either as capable of learning to direct his or her own life or as needing direction from others to determine appropriate goals and activities to fulfill society's expectations. These two streams of philosophical thought were evident in nineteenth- and twentieth-century approaches to the education of young children. Friedrick Froebel, father of the kindergarten concept, believed in a balance between an individual's freedom and society's responsibility to develop skills, knowledge, and values that allow the person to live in society. Froebel saw play as the natural way for children to learn and develop, and in his view the value of play depended on the amount of freedom children had to express their own aims and on their ability to carry out their own decisions.

John Dewey's philosophical pragmatism featured a child-centered education with the teacher as a stage setter, guide, and participant. Dewey believed that an individual's interests and abilities are the basis for education, that the child's potential is developed through social interaction, and that education is a continuing reconstruction of experience. Dewey believed that play should be based on realities and that children should be allowed free play according to their interests. Dewey emphasized "education for individuals" rather than individualistic education. Whereas individualistic education encourages competition through comparison for the comparatively few places at the top of the educational and social hierarchy, education for individuals develops each person according to his or her talents and interests as an equally valuable part of the social whole. As Dewey proposed, education that is based on moral principles "renders behavior more enlightened, more consistent and more vigorous than it would otherwise be."[1]

Another stream of thought was based on an emphasis upon observable behavior and the control of behavior. John B. Watson focused on predetermined mechanisms of stimulus and response. He proposed that parents and teachers could control the behavior of children strictly through reward and punishment methods. B. F. Skinner expanded behaviorism to describe the contingency and reinforcement schedules and proposed educational practices that would shape the behavior of children. The molecular view of behaviorists limited the conceptualization of the individual to one of objective data, thus curtailing the freedom of the individual to explore alternatives and to grow in unique and creative ways.

Humanistic psychology contributed a perspective that emphasized the pursuit of human potential and individual self-actualization. Carl Rogers's client-centered therapy described conditions that help each person become that "self which one truly is," through empathic acceptance, unconditional positive regard, and genuineness. Abraham Maslow's "hierarchy of needs" outlined the priorities given to basic needs for security and survival, love and respect, and self-actualization. Existentialist Rollo May emphasized individual yearning for transcendence and the guilt feelings that follow when potentials go unfulfilled. George Kelly focused on the cognitive processes by which individuals develop personal constructs of their interpersonal environment. Erik Erikson's "eight stages of man" have provided a comprehensive and popular conceptual framework for individual development. These psychological theories emphasize individual capacity for growth and development and suggest conditions that both block and strengthen such growth.

CONCEPTIONS OF INDIVIDUAL CHARACTERISTICS

Individuals have unique characteristics. Besides the obvious variations because of sex, age, ethnicity, and socioeconomic status, there are cognitive and affective characteristics that define each person. Much research has focused on the relationships among individual differences, educational practices, and learning. Within the limits imposed by this chapter, we take ego development, intellectual, moral and ethical development, self-concept and student development theory as key conceptual frameworks of individual differences.

Ego Development

Ego refers to that aspect of personality that strives for coherence and assigns meaning to experience. Adler's "style of life" equated self and ego with unity of personality, one's method of facing problems and one's attitude toward life. Ego development refers to "a sequence, cutting across chronological time, of interrelated patterns of cognitive, interpersonal and ethical development that form unified, successive and hierarchical world views."[2] A person's ego state is a pervasive, self-reinforcing frame of reference for experiencing the world and constitutes the personality framework in which learning is embedded. Instead of rigid, discrete steps of invariant sequence, stages of ego development can be viewed as gradations along a qualitative continuum, where the focus is on the dynamics of the transition from one stage to the next. Jane Loevinger described the stages of ego development and the accompanying milestone sequences. Each stage is a successive level of dealing with complexity as well as a broad character pattern involving impulse control, conscious preoccupations, interpersonal relationships, and cognitive styles.

Regarding the role that education has in promoting ego development, Erikson wrote: "Ego identity gains real strength only from wholehearted achievement that has meaning in our culture."[3] Nevitt Sanford said, "Anything that increases the likelihood that the sense of self will be based on personal experience rather than outside judgment favors the stabilization of ego identity . . . any situation that brings awareness of one's real preferences and inner continuities helps to establish ego identity."[4] Three basic conditions seem to foster ego development: (1) varied, direct experiences and roles, (2) meaningful achievement, and (3) relative freedom from anxiety and pressure. Education can provide each of these conditions.

Intellectual Development

Early "intelligence tests" provided psychologists with specific measures for assessing individual intellectual competence. Binet's omnibus test of intelligence confirmed Spearman's belief that all intellectual abilities reflected some common *g* factor that showed strong intercorrelations between measures of intellectual functions and predicted performance in most educational situations. Weschler's tests for children and adults further measured various components of intelligence and confirmed both Thurstone's hypothesis that intelligence involves several discrete factors and Guilford's structure of intellect model.

Crystallized abilities such as number facility, verbal comprehension, and general information processing depend on sociocultural factors, on a person's formal education in the formative years, and on vocational experiences and avocational activities during adulthood. Fluid abilities such as memory span, inductive reasoning, and spatial relations depend on genetic endowment, neurological structures, and incidental learning.

Table 5.1
Some Milestones of Ego Development

Stage	Impulse Control, Character Development	Interpersonal Style	Conscious Preoccupations	Cognitive Style
Impulsive	Impulsiveness, fear of retaliation	Receiving, dependent, exploitative	Bodily feelings, especially sexual and aggressive	
Self-Protective	Fear of being caught, externalization of blame, opportunism	Wary, manipulative, exploitative	Self-protection, trouble, wishes, things, advantage, control	Stereotyping, conceptual confusion
Conformist	Conformity to external rules, shame, guilt for breaking rules	Concerned with belonging, superficially nice	Appearance, social acceptability, banal feelings, behavior	Conceptual simplicity, stereotypes, clichés
Conscientious-Conformist (Self-Aware)	Differentiation of norms, goals	Aware of self in relation to group, helping	Adjustment, problems, reasons, opportunities (vague)	Multiplicity
Conscientious	Self-evaluated standards, self-criticism, guilt for consequences, long-term goals and labels	Intensive, responsible, mutual, concerned with communication	Differentiated feelings, motives for behavior, self-respect, achievements, traits, expression	Conceptual complexity, idea of patterning
Individualistic	*Add:* Respect for individuality	*Add:* Dependence as an emotional problem	*Add:* Development, social problems, differentiation of inner life from outer	*Add:* Distinction of process and outcome
Autonomous	*Add:* Coping with conflicting inner needs, toleration	*Add:* Respect for autonomy, interdependence	Vividly conveyed feelings, integration of physiological and psychological, psychological causation of behavior, role conception, self-fulfillment, self in social context	Increased conceptual complexity, complex patterns, toleration for ambiguity, broad scope, objectivity
Integrated	*Add:* Reconciling of inner conflicts, renunciation of unattainable	*Add:* Cherishing of individuality	*Add:* Identity	

Note: "*Add*" means in addition to the description applying to the previous level.

Source: Adapted from Loevinger, 1976, pp. 24-25.

Jean Piaget's monumental work emphasizes biologically based cognitive structures that produce qualitative changes in the way cognitive operations are conducted as the individual matures. William Perry has conceptualized and documented a hierarchical sequence of "positions" of intellectual and ethical development ranging from basic duality through multiplicity to relativism and commitment.

Moral and Ethical Development

Lawrence Kohlberg built on Piaget's empirical study of moral development as a part of cognitive development, using data from moral dilemmas, to identify six stages of moral development. With male adolescents as his main subjects, Kohlberg developed "education for justice" to combat the relativism of the times. He reconfirmed that principled morality depends upon the presence of underlying formal logical operations as posited by Piaget. Carol Gilligan examined Kohlberg's concepts as they applied to women. She found significant differences based on a greater concern for responsibility, caring, and relationships among women in contrast to the focus on justice and achievement posited by Kohlberg based on his studies of young men.

Conceptions Regarding Self

Several conceptions regarding self—phenomenal self, self-concept, sense of self, self-esteem and self-actualization—further illuminate our understanding of individual enhancement. Early in this century, William James included "self" as an important psychological construct. Gestalt psychology and research on human perception by Arthur Combs and Donald Snygg demonstrated that the maintenance and enhancement of the phenomenal self was the one basic human need. Self-concept according to Carl Rogers became defined as an organized configuration of perceptions of the self that are admissible to awareness. It is composed of elements such as perceptions of one's characteristics and abilities, of one's relation to others and the environment, and of one's values, goals, and ideals. An initial sense of self, "that I am," evolves later into "who I am." As Clark Moustakas wrote, "To the extent that [a person] respects the authenticity of his own experience, he will be open to new levels of learning, to new pathways of relating to others, and to genuine respect for all life."[5]

As self-concept becomes more positive, people generally feel better, and are able to function at higher levels and increase their options. Nathaniel Branden explained that self-esteem is the self-evaluation or value judgment one holds for one's self and is the conviction that one is competent to live and worthy of living; it is the integration of self-confidence and self-respect. Self-actualization, and tendency of the person to move toward achieving full potential, is at the pinnacle of Maslow's hierarchy of needs. Self-actualized individuals, who are committed to "Being" values, are creative in their total approach to life. The Humanizing Education movement led by Arthur Combs was heavily fueled by these conceptual perspectives. It gave prime attention to the "person in the process" and personal meanings became the objective of education.

Student Development Theory

Much developmental theory relating to adolescence and young adulthood has been formulated as "developmental tasks," "stages of development," "student typologies," and "needs and problem areas." Arthur Chickering synthesized much of this work in *Education and Identity* under seven major areas: competence, emotions, autonomy, identity, interpersonal relationships, purpose, and integrity. He called these conceptual clusters "vectors of development" because they seem to have both direction and magnitude.

Competence includes three major elements: intellectual competence, physical and manual skills, and social and interpersonal competence. Intellectual competence is pursued from childhood through college and influences professional and vocational alternatives chosen later. Physical and manual competence is important in terms of sports, athletics, dexterity, and the stamina to pursue life's tasks. Interpersonal competence is necessary because most life tasks require cooperative effort, while effectiveness generally depends upon the ability to work with others. In addition to these three elements, there is an overarching element called "sense of competence," the confidence one has in one's ability to cope with whatever comes and to achieve successfully what one sets out to do.

Managing emotions addresses the area of self-control and involves the ability to recognize and to manage sexual and aggressive impulses. Through increased awareness and through opportunities for self-expression and feedback, the student can achieve forms of expression appropriate to the circumstances.

Becoming autonomous includes emotional and instrumental independence, and recognizing one's interdependence. Emotional independence occurs when one is free from continual and pressing needs for reassurance, affection, or approval from parents, peers, and others. Instrumental independence occurs when one has the ability to carry on activities and to cope with problems without seeking help and the ability to be mobile in relation to one's needs and desires. Recognition and acceptance of interdependence is the capstone of autonomy.

Establishing identity for the young adult is more than the aggregate of change in competence, emotions, and autonomy. As Erikson said, identity is "the accrued confidence that one's ability to maintain inner sameness and continuity is matched by the sameness and continuity of one's meaning for others."[6] Identity involves clarifying conceptions concerning physical needs and characteristics, personal appearance, sexual identification, sex roles and behavior. A solid sense of identity fosters change in the other three vectors of interpersonal relationships, purpose, and integrity.

Developing freer interpersonal relationships involves increased tolerance and increased capacity to respond to persons in their own right rather than as stereotypes. Friendship and love relationships shift toward greater trust, independence, individuality, and intimacy and can survive differences and disagreements.

Development of purpose occurs as questions of "Who am I going to be?" and "Where am I going?" are answered with increasing clarity and conviction. Development of purpose requires formulating plans and priorities that integrate vocational plans and aspirations, avocational and recreational interests, and general lifestyle considerations. As Chickering concluded, "With such integration, life flows with direction and meaning."[7]

Developing integrity entails forming a personally valid set of beliefs that have some internal consistency and that provide tentative guides for behavior. Such development involves the humanizing of values, the personalizing of values, and the development of congruence. Robert White described the humanizing of values as the shift from a literal belief in the absoluteness of rules to a more relative view. Connections are made between rules and the purposes they are meant to serve and thus a shift from the internalization of one's parents' values to one's own. Personalizing of values leads to the development of congruence or the achievement of behavior consistent with the personalized values held. These seven vectors of student development apply to late adolescents and young adults and to many older adults returning to college who find themselves confronted with these important issues at a different level.

EDUCATIONAL PRACTICES

Educational practices to enhance individual development have been tested and pursued throughout this century by many educational leaders and in many different contexts. We address the relevant practices under the general rubrics of Individualized Education, Experiential Learning, and Evaluation. These educational practices are accompanied by different types of relationships between students and teachers and among students.

Individualized Education

Individualized education encompasses a wide range of educational practices: individually guided education, discovery education, mastery learning, personalized systems of instruction, open education, and contract learning. These diverse practices share the common characteristic of recognizing one or more dimensions of individual differences, in pacing or timing, in content emphases, in outcomes or products, in methods or criteria for evaluation, or in student motivation or objectives.

Education is most "individualized" in the home. Parents, grandparents, and siblings teach infants and young children informally in idiosyncratic ways. Through admonitions, rules, expectations, and modeling, children are taught to become members of the family and the larger society. Through this informal education children gain a sense of self, other people, the community, and the larger world. They acquire values and develop diverse intellectual competencies and manual skills depending upon the family setting and parental disposition. When children enter the formal educational system at nursery school, kindergarten, or elementary school, they encounter a world, a "life space" where others' assumptions and expectations determine what is to be learned, when, where, and how.

Individually Guided Education (IGE). Developed by Herbert Klausmeier, this alternative to the age-graded, self-contained classroom, accounts for level of achievement at the start, rate of progress, learning style, and motivation. A comprehensively designed system, IGE includes (1) an individually developed instructional program in which each child learns at his or her own rate, (2) instructional materials to accommodate to individual learning styles, (3) large group, small group, independent study, and one-to-one instruction to suit each child's best learning style, and (5) matching of students with teachers who can best help for specific learning tasks.

Discovery Education. Jerome Bruner argued that good teaching requires that students discover knowledge for themselves. He held that there is nothing mysterious about this act. It is a matter of re-arranging or transforming data in such a way that one is helped to go beyond the evidence to acquire new insights. As opposed to an expository mode, he proposed a hypothetical mode in which the teacher and student collaborate in formulating hypotheses, the student often taking the principal role. Then together they seek to confirm or disconfirm the hypotheses. The benefits of the discovery method included (1) an increase in intellectual potency, (2) a shift from extrinsic to intrinsic rewards, (3) the learning of heuristics of discovery, and (4) the aid to conserving memory. Discovery education allowed students, especially in the field of science, to explore new concepts and discover truth for themselves. This approach empowered the individual by fostering basic strategies for problem identification and learning.

In higher education this approach characterized good teaching in other natural sciences where laboratory experiments test real hypotheses using methods that often generate ambiguous outcomes. Unfortunately, much laboratory work follows a more cookbook approach where students follow a set of directions that lead to highly predictable results. This procedure may familiarize students with the rudiments of the scientific method and with some basic techniques, but it does not tap into fundamental inquiry processes and the excitement of discovery that can occur in the context of real hypothesis formation and testing. Of course, the most powerful expression of discovery education occurs when students are active collaborators in faculty research projects, whether these be experimental laboratory studies, behavioral science research, or scholarly inquiries in the arts and humanities. The educational power of this kind of shared exploration has been demonstrated at the Massachusetts Institute of Technology, Brown Univeristy, and at a small number of other colleges that have developed well-organized programs for student participation in faculty research.

Mastery Learning/Personalized Systems of Instruction. Mastery learning and Personalized Systems of Instruction (PSI) assume that individual differences in learning outcomes are largely a function of the amount of time different students need in order to learn materials at various levels of difficulty. Another assumption is that agreement can be reached on what is to be learned, on what the appropriate sequences of knowledge or competence should be, and on the criteria appropriate for mastery of the material. These approaches postulate that all or most students can reach the same level of mastery if they are allowed to work at their own pace and timing and if they are given adequate diagnostic feedback about their strengths and weaknesses and about the accuracy or error of their responses. Subject matter is divided into clearly defined units that cover one lesson on a single concept or competence and that taken together encompass a clearly defined subject matter area or set of skills. Students are tested at the end of each unit. If they meet the criteria for mastery, they proceed to the next unit. If they do not, they receive information about the flaws in their performance, undertake further study, or receive special assistance. When ready, they take the test again.

This approach has been used at elementary and secondary levels and in undergraduate education as well. Most frequently it has been employed in the natural sciences and mathematics, less frequently in the behavioral sciences, and seldom in the humanities. Evaluative research has dominated strong achievement effects under mastery conditions. It is not uncommon for 75 to 90 percent of the students to achieve mastery under this approach compared with rates of 10 to 25 percent for students in traditional classes. At Rockland Community College in Suffern, New York, for example, rates for successful completion of mathematics courses jumped from 20 to 80 percent after a mastery learning alternative was created.

Open Education. Open Education or "Open Plan" education postulates that children learn in different ways at different times from things around them that interest them. The teacher acts as guide, facilitator, and resource person and encourages pupils to proceed at their own pace and develop independence of thought. The goal is to develop initiative, creativity, and critical thinking. In studies comparing open and traditional classrooms, the number and complexity of variables involved almost preclude definitive findings. Generally, results for open classrooms indicated improvement in cognitive areas, but little statistically significant difference in other areas. The success of the open school appears to depend heavily on the persons in the school who plan, organize, and implement the curriculum.

The counterparts to "Open Education" in undergraduate and graduate education are found in various "Alternative Degree" programs. These programs start with each student's purposes and background. Based on the student's purposes, an individual degree program is planned that meets institutional criteria for content requirements, internships, theses, dissertations, or other requirements. The timing, location, and educational resources employed are treated flexibly in response to each student's work and life realities. Typically, full-time core faculty members serve as mentors, resource persons, and monitors of student progress. They are usually supplemented by other part-time faculty members who have expertise pertinent to the particular student's program. This team has responsibility for assuring the quality of the work done in the program, for reading and approving papers and examinations, and for supervising or approving internships and other key institutional requirements.

This approach, which began in a serious way in the early 1960s, has gathered momentum in higher education during the 1970s and 1980s. There are now fully accredited undergraduate and graduate programs in all regions of the country. These programs have been developed as additional alternatives by public and private colleges and universities such as New College at the University of Alabama, the University College at Memphis State University, and the Adult Degree programs at Goddard College, Mary Baldwin College, Millsaps College, and elsewhere. Institutions created specifically in this mode include Empire State College as part of the State University of New York system, Metropolitan State College as part of the University of Minnesota system, and private institutions such as the Fielding Institute and the Union for Experimenting Colleges and Universities.

Contract Learning. Contract Learning is an instructional counterpart to open learning. Open learning typically describes general educational orientations, environments, and systems that respond to individual differences in student purposes and backgrounds. These alternative approaches often employ learning contracts as the building blocks for different units of study that comprise the individually designed degree programs. The power of contract learning comes from the opportunity it provides to individualize all the major elements of the learning process: purposes, educational activities, pacing and total time, methods and criteria for evaluation, experiential activities, and academic studies. This approach lets both the student and the faculty member take into account the general background, ability level, and working knowledge of the student when the contract is designed. Student strengths and weaknesses can be recognized and dealt with directly or compensated for depending upon the contract purposes. Both student and faculty member can try to optimize the level of challenge and range of activities in response to the student's preferred learning style and in response to the requirements of the content or competence to be acquired.

A learning contract typically includes a statement of purposes, the learning activities to be pursued, the educational resources to be used in terms of books, faculty expertise, or experiential learning activities, and a description of the products or outcomes to be evaluated together with agreed-upon criteria for the evaluation. Some learning contract formats ask students to distinguish between long-range or general goals and the specific purposes of the contract. Often they also call for pretesting or include a description of the knowledge and competence pertinent to the contract already acquired by the student. Thus, a sound contract typically includes five major elements:

1. Purposes: The long-range goals and specific purposes, both stated in terms of learning outcomes

2. Antecedent Status: A description of the student's prior experiences and current knowledge or competence pertinent to contract goals, based on prior assessments or on evaluation during the contract planning process

3. Learning Activities: The processes to be pursued and the products to be created designed to foster the outcomes indicated by the purposes

4. Educational Resources: The readings, consultations, field experiences, and human expertise to be employed as part of the learning activities

5. Evaluation: The evidences to be supplied for evaluation, the methods to be used, and the criteria to be applied

Contract learning has been used most frequently in nontraditional institutions characterized by the open learning approach described above. It is being increasingly used with traditional students in traditional institutions because of its adaptability and positive results with diverse students. It is also increasingly used in regular courses in combination with a shared core of activities that all students pursue. This adaptation of contract learning to courses and classes of varying sizes adds an instructional modality that can be employed throughout the curriculum to powerful effect. When students have an opportunity to address their own purposes and negotiate their own learning activities and evaluation within the context of a group study, motivation is enhanced, energy is released, and learning that relates to student concerns is enhanced.

Experiential Learning. "A burned child dreads the fire." "Practice makes perfect." "Experience is the best teacher." "Experiential learning" is our current jargon for an educational philosophy and associated practices that have a long history in our schools and colleges, particularly among those oriented to enhancing individual development. Indeed, prior to the advent of formal schooling, education and training were almost entirely "experiential." From the medieval period through the industrial revolution, craft guilds and apprenticeship systems were the chief modes of advanced training. Concurrently, the education of the elite was carried out through the various chivalric traditions. As Houle reminds us, that system was highly "experiential" and "competency based." He describes some of the required competencies:

> The squire must be able to: Spring upon a horse while fully armed; to exercise himself in running; to strike for a length of time with the axe or club; to dance and do somersaults fully armed except for his helmet; to mount on horseback behind one of his comrades, by barely laying his hands on his sleeve; to raise himself betwixt two partition walls to any height . . . to mount a ladder . . . upon the reverse or underside, solely by the aid of his hands . . . to throw the javelin; and to pitch the bar.

Chaucer's squire in *Canterbury Tales* reminds us how the humanities and performing arts accompanied these professional/vocational skills:

> He could make songs and poems and recite,
> Knew how to joust, to dance, to draw, to write.
> He loved so hotly that when dawn grew pale
> He'd slept as little as a nightingale.
> Courteous he was, and humble, willing, able;
> He carved to serve his father at the table.[8]

In those days, as today, nonformal learning activities provided a rich background for more formal efforts. Libraries, museums, churches, and courts provided resources and events. Annual feasts and festivals carried cultures and taught traditions. Wandering minstrels, storytellers, and itinerant tradesmen brought news, myths, and word of other lands. The local pub, inn, and village green provided meeting grounds to exchange common wisdom, examine current practices, and test new ideas.

Then came the industrial revolution. Factories replaced craftsmen, unions replaced guilds, job simplification reduced complex tasks to easily learned skills. The university increasingly emphasized content and authority and rejected direct experiences and useful applications. But in the United States counterpressures mounted for a university education that was practical as well as theoretical to meet the needs of the new frontiers in agriculture, engineering, architecture, and forestry. The land-grant colleges evolved in the late 1900s at about the same time that the natural sciences were finally given curricular recognition at Cambridge and Oxford.

Then came John Dewey's seminal contribution that still stands as the best expression of an educational philosophy that integrates experience and learning with a concern for individual development. Dewey's thinking was grounded in the assumption of an "organic connection between education and personal experience." His words are as timely today as they were when he wrote *Experience and Education* in 1938.

> If one attempts to formulate the philosophy of education implicit in the practices of the new education, we may, I think, discover certain common principles. . . . To imposition from above is opposed expression and cultivation of individuality; to external discipline is opposed free activity; to learning from texts and teachers, learning through experience; to acquisition of isolated skills and techniques by drill is opposed acquisition of them as means of attaining ends which make direct vital appeal; to preparation for a more or less remote future is opposed making the most of the opportunities of present life; to static aims and materials is opposed acquaintance with a changing world. . . . When external control is rejected, the problem becomes that of finding the factors of control that are inherent within the experience. . . . When external authority is rejected, it does not follow that all authority should be rejected, but rather that there is a need to search for a more effective source of authority. Because the older education imposed the knowledge, methods, and the rules of conduct . . . it does not follow . . . that the knowledge and skill of the mature person have no directive value for the experience of the immature. On the contrary, basing education upon personal experience may mean more multiplied and more intimate contacts between the mature and the immature than ever existed in the traditional schools, and consequently more, rather than less, guidance by others.[9]

These thoughts express fundamental propositions that still hold true for experiential learning. In elementary and secondary schools, this orientation is most often expressed through student projects, field trips, community volunteer work, and other activities that provide vehicles for developing basic competencies and for understanding key issues in history, social studies, and the sciences. Several of the strategies discussed above concerning individualized education—individually guided education, discovery learning, open education, and contract learning—are rooted in Dewey's basic principles, as they take each learner's purposes and interests as the point of departure for designing and carrying out educational programs.

In colleges and universities, in addition to classroom projects and laboratory activities that aim to supplement reading, writing, and discussion with concrete experiences and applications, a variety of field experience programs have been developed. Duley and Gordon have identified eleven major categories:

1. *Cooperative education* integrates classroom experiences and practical work experiences in industrial, business, government, or service settings. These work experiences are a regular element of the educational program and minimum standards are set for successful performance.

2. *Career or occupational development programs* help students identify a series of two or more placements that are chosen to advance skills or perspectives pertinent to a specific career.

3. *Career exploration* provides placement in order to perform a useful service to the host organization or profession, to analyze the career possibilities of that placement, and to develop employment-related skills. The educational institution provides the resources for structured reflection, analysis, and self-evaluation while the field supervisor provides an evaluation of the student's work and career potential.

4. *Preprofessional training* gives students explicit responsibilities carried out under the supervision of professionals, typically in education, medicine, law, social work, nursing, or the ministry, thereby putting theory into practice and strengthening appropriate professional skills.

5. *Institutional analysis* provides opportunities to develop skills or to test abilities and career interests by systematically examining institutional cultures using theoretical concepts from a chosen academic field.

6. *Academic discipline/career integration* serves students who have been employed in business, government, industry, a service organization or profession prior to entry into the educational institution. Faculty members and the institution provide analyses and evaluation based on appropriately related academic disciplines to integrate theory and practice and help the student understand prior experiences in a more conscious and systematic fashion.

7. *Service learning internships* integrate accomplishing some specific task which meets a human need with specific objectives for educational growth, typically carried out within a public or private institution.

8. *Field research/participation in the arts* helps students undertake an independent or group research project under faculty supervision applying the concepts and methods of an academic discipline such as archeology, geology, psychology, sociology, or geography. Similar activities occur in the performing or graphic arts under the guidance of qualified professionals.

9. *Social/political action* provides opportunities to work directly in the social or political arenas through community organizing, political campaigning, research and action programs, or work with organizations seeking to bring about social change.

10. *Personal growth and development* involves off-campus activities such as wilderness survival programs, apprenticeships, residence in a house of a religious order, or participation in group psychological or human relations programs, where the object is intentional pursuit of one or more issues concerning personal growth and development.

11. *Cross-cultural experiences* involve students in another culture or in a subculture of the home society in a significant way, as a family member, worker, volunteer, or participant observer, in order to learn as much as possible about that culture, and through reflection, about one's culture of origin.[10]

A diverse range of pedagogical styles are used in these programs. Faculty roles include providing information; acting as mentor, supervisor, and evaluator; identifying and designing learning environments; acting as facilitator, trainer, consultant, resource person, and colleague. Students' roles include assimilating information and receiving instruction; applying knowledge and skill under supervision; designing and carrying out independent or collaborative research and action projects; developing self-understanding, interpersonal competence, problem identification, and problem-solving skills; identifying and documenting learning outcomes. This range of pedagogical styles, faculty roles, and student roles can meet a wide range of individual needs and areas for personal development. Overcoming the artificial barriers between concrete experience and abstract concepts, between personal reflection and active application and experimentation can powerfully enhance education for personal development.

Mediated Instruction

Mediated instruction provides the possibility of meeting individual learning needs more effectively than are presently being met through face-to-face communication between teacher and student. The resources for mediated instruction include print, xerography, microfiche, correspondence, telephone, radio, film, video, television, and the computer. Print is the most widely used technique of mediated instruction and remains the most cost-effective of all media. The Carnegie Commission on Higher Education in 1972 hailed the new technology as the "Fourth Revolution" and predicted that by the year 2000 a significant proportion of instruction would be delivered through informational technology and may become the single greatest opportunity for change on and off campus.

Computers are certainly having an impact on education; however, the revolution appears to be quieter than previously predicted. Complex programming that provides branching to fill gaps in required information or skills to deal with typical misunderstandings can also recognize differences in ability or prior learning. The opportunities for individualized learning experiences through computer-based education are infinite and limited only by time and the imagination of those in charge and by the response from the public.

Earlier in this century, radio had been particularly useful in education in rural settings. However, it is now television that has widespread general acceptance for informal learning with programs such as "Sesame Street," "The Ascent of Man," "Nature," and "Masterpiece Theater" contributing significantly to the learning of the young and the mature. Many colleges offer television courses through the National University Consortium and other outlets for distant learners, including both the homebound and working adults, in order to meet individualized learning needs.

Education for Handicapped Persons

Education for handicapped persons at all levels has greatly affected the delivery of individualized instruction. Public Law 94-192, The Education for All Handicapped Children Act, and the federal regulations implementing Section 504 of the Rehabilitation Act of 1973 have required the provision of instruction to meet the needs of children with disabilities. Some of the language of the law speaks directly to individualization and respect for differences.

- Each handicapped child requires an educational blueprint custom-tailored to achieve his/her maximum potential
- Assurance of special education being provided to all handicapped children in the least restrictive environment
- Assurance of the maintenance of an individualized program for all handicapped children
- Assurance of an effective policy guaranteeing the right of all handicapped children to a free, appropriate education.

Nicholas Hobbs addressed the assumptions underlying the need for special education for exceptional children and especially for public policy:

Public and private policies and practices must manifest respect for the individuality of children and appreciation of the positive value of their individual talents and diverse cultural backgrounds. Classification procedures must not be used to violate this fundamental social value.

The richness and vitality of our national life will not be enhanced by increased uniformity, by the imposition on all children of the values and aspirations of the dominant, white, Anglo-Saxon, Protestant majority. To the extent that classification and labeling serve this end, as they sometimes do, they are suspect. Public policy should manifest a commitment to cultural pluralism, to the appreciation of enriching values to be found in the ways of life of people of diverse ethnic and racial backgrounds. Public policy should support the right of the individual to be different, and encourage not mere tolerance but a positive valuing of difference.[11]

Chickering and Chickering proposed an amendment to P.L. 94-192 that would replace the words "handicapped children" with the word "persons" to encompass all and to extend the concept to lifelong learning. The basic principles of educating handicapped children are those that underlie all effective teaching and learning and are entirely consistent with fundamentally sound principles for education for all.

Evaluation

The history of elementary, secondary, and higher education in the United States can be thought of as a constant effort to provide more and better education for a wider range of the total population. Our constitutional democracy and national ideals provide constant pressures driving us to move from an aristocratic tradition where education was reserved for the elite, through a meritocratic orientation where education is for the best and the brightest, to an egalitarian orientation where all persons regardless of race, religion, national origin, family background, or preexisting handicap are entitled to a fair and publicly supported education. That egalitarian orientation calls not simply for equality of access to elementary, secondary, and higher education but also for equality of opportunities to succeed, to learn, to develop the knowledge and competence necessary for work, for satisfactory human relationships, and for effective citizenship. Though great progress has been made, that marvelous aspiration remains to be achieved, even at the levels of elementary and secondary education. Our limited success stems not so much from limited commitment as from the fact that our competence and our resources are continually outrun by increasing cultural pluralism and student diversity, and by the increasingly complex demands from the worlds of work, human relationships, and citizenship. If we enjoyed the cultural homogeneity of most Western European countries, and if the growth rates for new knowledge, the life expectancy and work-life expectancy, the employment alternatives, and the rate of new job formation had remained like those of the early twentieth century, then the competence and knowledge of our high school and college graduates would surely better approximate our social needs. But the race goes on apace and who can say whether we are gaining or losing ground.

Perhaps the part of our educational enterprise most sorely challenged by these sharp increases in cultural pluralism and increasing complexity is evaluation. Figure 1 illustrates the problem as it is experienced in higher education. As college and university admissions counselors are well aware, the same conditions exist for secondary schools in every city, state, and region.

The top curves give the mean, standard deviations and distribution curves for the ACT national data and for Tennessee state-supported two- and four-year institutions. The bottom curves give the same data

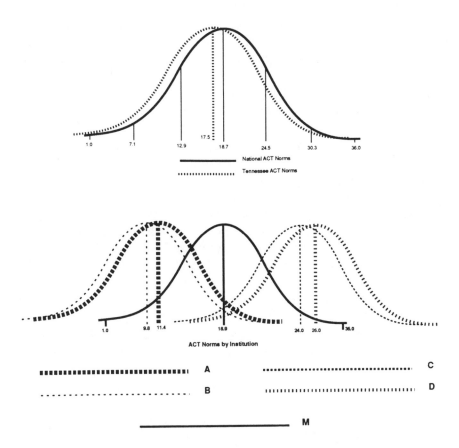

Figure 5.1
National, State and Institutional Distribution of ACT Scores

for five Memphis higher education institutions. Students are clearly sorted by ACT scores among these institutions. Each institution establishes its own normative framework for evaluation and grading. Within each institution students receive A's, B's, C's, D's and F's. Consequently, students in some institutions receive A's and B's for performances that are graded D or F in another institution, and vice versa. At the same time, there is relatively easy transfer among these institutions for courses or degree programs successfully completed.

Given this diversity, the meaning of the evaluation at each institution becomes parochial in the extreme. The normative frameworks for evaluation, and the grading curves used, bear little relationship to any clear or shared indices of performance. Even within each institution those indices are seldom clearly defined or stable. During the late 1950s and early 1960s in many higher education institutions, the grading curves remained stable while the ability levels of students increased markedly. Thus in a four- to six-year period the ACT or SAT average for entering students rose substantially in those institutions able to be more and more selective, but roughly the same proportions of students received grades A through F. Now that process is being reversed. Entering test scores are dropping at many institutions, but the grading curves remain about the same. Back in the fifties Paul Dressel said that a grade is an inadequate report, of an inaccurate judgment, by a biased and variable judge, of the extent to which a student has attained an undefined level of mastery, of an unknown proportion, of an indefinite amount of material. Unfortunately, that description is probably as accurate today as it was then.

In most comprehensive universities there will be different distributions of academic ability among the different colleges. Similar differences will exist among programs in comprehensive secondary schools. If there are significant differences, does it make sense to assume that the same desired grade distribution should apply to all program areas? And if it is applied, what then do the grades mean in terms of some clear index of quality or performance? If we adopt a single normative standard across the diverse range of students served by a university or high school, then we will be failing many students who would merit B's and C's at other institutions, and we will be giving A's and B's to students who would merit only C's and D's elsewhere. If we use a normative approach but establish different standards for program areas or for subgroups within a particular institution, we reinforce the perception of the first-, second-, and third-class credentials, hardly a direction we want to pursue.

Institutions oriented toward enhancing individual potential have tried to address this problem in a number of ways. Their responses typically involve a combination of several ingredients. They try to recognize a wide range of learning as educationally legitimate.

K. Patricia Cross, professor at the Harvard School of Education, puts it this way:

> We know that on any single dimension of human ability half of the students in the nation will be below average. Naive egalitarians have the notion that working with the bottom half will somehow raise them to equal status with the top half. Well, unfortunately, status in the society is relative, and on any single measure there will always be a lower half. The only way to reduce the number in the lower half is to expand the number of dimensions along which talent is measured.[12]

Today, together with a concern for the solid development of basic skills, there is a widely recognized need to expand the range of student purposes and human potentials served by education. To the extent that education responds to these wide-ranging needs society is enriched by diversity, and the possibilities for individual contribution, self-expansion and self-satisfaction are increased. Schools and colleges responding to these needs are recognizing a diverse set of educational purposes, be they particular intellectual, vocational, or professional skills, knowledge and competence pertinent to various social problems, broader areas of intellectual competence, or more general dimensions of interpersonal competence and personal development. Then they help each student clarify his or her major areas for effort and develop clearly articulated standards for performance in those areas. These program plans and criteria then become the basis for evaluation. These institutions avoid a general normative approach and set standards that are sound for each combination of individual abilities and program purposes. They spell out the criteria for performance at different levels of excellence or acceptability and develop assessment procedures that address those different levels. Their teaching practices not only aim to cover specific content areas but also to explicitly use the content areas as vehicles for encouraging the specific competencies or skills required by the program. The outcomes of the assessment and evaluation processes are typically not confined to a single letter grade or number but provide substantive feedback concerning strengths and weaknesses, accurate responses, and errors. Narrative statements often replace or supplement letter or numerical grades on internal records and on transcripts sent to other institutions.

Most importantly, these institutions tackle the problem of assessing gain, of evaluating how much learning actually occurs rather than simply testing student status at the end of a course, program of studies, or degree. They recognize that the quality of their education really rests on how much learning and personal development they help students accomplish, the "value added" to each student's store of competence and working knowledge, which occurs as a consequence of the teaching practices and educational experiences they provide. This assessment occurs not only at the level of evaluating individual student performance but also at the level of general program evaluation. They have taken seriously the view that, if they are to respond to increased demands for accountability and if they are to do right by their students, they must develop procedures for teaching and evaluation that recognize wide-ranging individual differences in student backgrounds and purposes that recognize the diverse types of knowledge, competence, and personal characteristics required by the complex learning and information society in which we live.

Faculty Roles and Student Relationships

Educational approaches to enhance personal purposes and individual development call for new faculty roles and student relationships. The emphasis on these roles varies with the particular approach used but most roles are required in some degree. The role of mentor/counselor/facilitator is a key one in open education, contract learning, and in experiential learning settings. It is impossible to avoid a heavy emphasis on this role when helping students clarify their purposes, identify learning activities, and make judgments about the methods and criteria for evaluation. Discussion of long-range goals and specific contract purposes frequently raises larger questions concerning meaning and direction and requires students to confront implications for their current life-style, personal relationships, future plans and aspirations. Most college and university faculty members and secondary teachers are not well prepared for this role or comfortable with it. This lack of readiness is a major obstacle to the widespread development of such educational alternatives. Significant investments in professional development are required if such approaches are to become a substantial part of our national educational enterprise.

The broker/negotiator role is closely allied to the mentor/counselor/facilitator role. Open education and contract learning are by definition rarely prescriptive. Experiential learning is by nature rich and complex and thus difficult to evaluate. Giving up norm-referenced evaluation and developing criterion-referenced, individualized approaches with narrative transcripts can feel like stepping from granite to quicksand. Yet institutions and individual faculty members do have their requirements or expectations, sometimes clearly articulated, more often left abstract and vague. To reach agreement between student and faculty member, student and faculty committee, student and institutional degree program requirements, requires a sometimes subtle and sometimes hard-nosed negotiation of differences. Faculty do have responsibility for assuring the quality of student performance and that function cannot be exercised if faculty abdicate responsibility for being clear about institutional requirements and their own expectations. This area is often the soft spot in educational programs to enhance individual development. The quality of education frequently stands or falls on the degree to which this broker/negotiator role is effectively managed.

The traditional instructor/tutor role is also present. This role is often exercised in ways quite different from typical classroom teaching. One is more often asking key questions, drawing together insights from diverse sources, suggesting particular strategies for learning difficult subject matter or for strengthening weak areas. The evaluator role is also present but exercised in a different way, either in relation to the mastery levels specified in advance or in relation to the criteria and evidences agreed upon in open education and contract learning approaches. This role interacts powerfully with the broker/negotiator role. If agreements concerning desired outcomes and the methods and criteria for evaluation are well articulated at the outset, then evaluation can be similarly sound and clear. If, on the other hand, the initial negotiations are vague or absent, then evaluation becomes slippery and highly subjective.

All these approaches to education for individual development require that the teacher create instructional materials or identify and make accessible a wide range of learning resources. Discovery education, mastery learning, personalized systems of instruction and their kin all require heavy investments of faculty time preparing appropriate instructional materials. Issues of sequencing, difficulty levels, learning resources, methods and criteria for evaluation all have to be spelled out in detail and appropriate materials have to be prepared in advance before the first student begins. These are typically refined with experience but the up-front work required can be daunting. Open education and contract learning do not call for detailed, prestructured learning programs, resources, and evaluation materials but instead require access to a wide range of diverse settings for experiential learning, access to good libraries, and access to broad-gauged human expertise. Most learning contracts and degree programs do not fit our preordained disciplinary boxes. They tend to be interdisciplinary, multidisciplinary, thematic, or problem oriented. They require unique combinations of resource materials for different learners. The teacher needs to be knowledgeable about those varied resources and able to help the student use them in ways that address the purposes and produce the desired outcomes.

These roles are new for most higher education faculty members and secondary teachers. Most persons who have become competent with these educational approaches have learned on the job, pulling themselves along by their own bootstraps, taking the added effort out of their own hides. Typically, they have substantial help from students, formally and informally, as they learn through experience, trial and error, successes and failures. Most institutions that develop such programs establish ongoing professional development programs in which faculty members and their administrative colleagues share experiences, provide advice and counsel, and offer emotional support as that learning occurs. Such programs should be a key ingredient for any institution that would move significantly toward enhancing individual development.[13]

These varied approaches to individualized education typically foster relationships among students that differ from those which characterize typical courses, classes, and curricula. Because evaluation tends to be criterion referenced rather than norm referenced or because evaluation is related to each person's particular purposes and learning activities, the competitive pressures associated with group instruction and norm-referenced evaluation are much reduced. The payoffs from collaborative efforts, from working together, from helping one another identify good books, faculty expertise, useful field experiences, strategies for acquiring and retaining key concepts or competencies are significantly enhanced. Thus supportive, cooperative, sharing work relationships tend to characterize students involved in these varied approaches to individualized education much more than is the case with traditional group instruction.

These varied educational practices which respond to each student's personal purposes and which aim to enhance individual development have a long history in elementary, secondary, and higher education. When they have been pursued with integrity and implemented with rigor, they have proven highly effective. By now there is an accumulation of solid research evidence documenting their educational power, reaching back to the Eight Year Study of progressive education and to Newcomb's landmark study of Bennington College, both carried out during the late 1930s, and continuing with major multi-institutional longitudinal research projects during the 1960s, 1970s and early 1980s. The internal consistency among these findings unequivocally supports the educational power of approaches that share seven major ingredients:

1. They respect individual students and take their purposes and their backgrounds seriously.
2. They create educational programs based on those purposes and on the backgrounds of the students.
3. They involve significant investments in experiential learning as part of regular classroom activities and through off-campus or out-of-school settings.
4. They establish solid standards based on clear institutional requirements and faculty expectations.
5. They evaluate student learning in relation to criteria pertinent to each student's purposes and to institutional requirements.
6. They put students and faculty members in collaborative, collegial relationships where faculty members are mentors, models, or resource persons.
7. They encourage collaborative learning and cooperative efforts among students.

CONCLUSION

Despite the accumulated evidence concerning the power of educational environments that share these characteristics, there continues to be an historical ebb and flow throughout our educational system of an emphasis on individual enhancement as the personal purpose of education. During some periods, enhancing individual development, trying to address the "whole child," is emphasized. Other periods focus on the "basics," on reading, writing, arithmetic, on "the intellect" alone, and emphasize straightforward knowledge acquisition and information transfer.

The tension between the forces pushing for socialization and conformity and the forces encouraging individualism and pluralism can be viewed from a macrosystemic viewpoint. Historically, conformity issues have been in the forefront (a) when there was increased immigration, such as at the turn of the century, (b) when there have been national emergencies, such as wars, depressions, and recessions, and (c) when there have been threats to our political freedoms, such as McCarthyism and Sputnik. Trends toward encouraging individualism seem to have occurred more during periods of economic affluence, such as during the 1920s and the late 1960s and early 1970s.

Perhaps Maslow's hierarchy of needs provides an effective template for viewing these interactions between cultural conditions and educational orientations. During periods of threat, our entire society is operating at lower levels of the hierarchy; individuals are working for survival and the satisfaction of basic needs. These political and economic forces demand conformity. Education responds by focusing instrumentally on survival needs with "back to basics" programs. Conversely, during periods of economic affluence, many people are exploring higher order needs, striving for acceptance, moving toward self-actualization. Such prevailing forces allow individuals to be more self-expressive and to seek self-fulfillment. Then education encourages individual self-exploration and provides opportunities for individual growth. Daniel Yankelovich portrayed the 1970 recession following the world oil crisis as a "search for new rules in a world turned upside down," as a reaction after the flower child era of the 1960s. With the recent economic prosperity of the mid-1980s, education is again moving toward valuing liberal arts, strengthening broader dimensions of human competence and motivation, and calling for student involvement.

These shifting orientations affect educational practices and professional development. Even though the dominant educational modality historically has been socialization for life and work, there are ways to strengthen opportunities on the side of individual enhancement. Such practices and policies for strengthening the individual might include:

1. Helping individuals to increase self-awareness. Provide information about personality characteristics, human development, learning styles, purposes and values. The more meaningful information one has, the more self-aware one can be.

2. Helping individuals learn how to learn. Teach learning skills so that students can take charge of their own learning.

3. Helping individuals develop self-confidence. Find ways to help students become successful, to gain a sense of competence and autonomy, and to realize their own potential.

4. Recognizing and respecting individual differences. Teach that being different and unique optimizes our cultural pluralism.

Research agendas flow from these educational imperatives. What kinds of information help individuals become more self-aware? What are effective ways to teach individuals *how* to learn in addition to *what* to learn? What educational practices help individuals gain self-confidence and to feel successful? How can individual differences best be recognized, and what behaviors constitute respect for individual differences?

Although individual differences have been studied extensively by psychologists and educators, there is a need for more research and for greater utilization of research in improving educational practices. The outcomes of research could be designed to address more specifically the goals of the individual instead of exclusively addressing institutional or societal goals.

Where does this lead us for the last decade of the twentieth century? When future educational historians review the contributions of the century, will their overriding verdict be that the forces for socialization and conformity outweighed the forces for individualization and pluralism? Let us hope that twentieth-century education will be seen as contributing to the enhancement of the individual and as recognizing the personal purpose of education for each individual. If we do so, we will create an involved citizenry, a competent work force, rich human relationships among parents and children, friends and loved ones, and individuals strong in identity and integrity.

NOTES

1. John Dewey, *Moral Principles in Education* (Boston: Houghton Mifflin, 1909), p. 3.

2. Rita P. Weathersby, "Today's Students and Their Needs," in *The Modern American College* ed. A. W. Chickering and associates (San Francisco: Jossey-Bass, Inc., 1981), p. 52.

3. Erik H. Erikson, *Identity, Youth and Crisis* (New York: W. W. Norton & Co., 1968), p. 135.

4. Nevitt Sanford, "The Developmental Status of the Entering Freshman," in *The American College*, ed. N. Sanford (New York: John Wiley & Sons, 1962), p. 281.

5. Clark Moustakas, *Creativity and Conformity* (Princeton, N.J.: D. Van Nostrand Co., 1967), p. 13.

6. Erik H. Erikson, *Childhood and Society* (New York: W. W. Norton & Co., 1950), p. 135.

7. Arthur W. Chickering, *Education and Identity* (San Francisco: Jossey-Bass, Inc., 1969), p. 17.

8. Cyrie O. Houle, "Deep Traditions of Experiential Learning," in *Experiential Learning* ed. M. T. Keeton and associates (San Francisco: Jossey-Bass, Inc., 1976), pp. 23-24.

9. John Dewey, *Experience and Education* (New York: Collier Books, 1963), pp. 19-21.

10. John Duley and Shelia Gordon, *College-Sponsored Experiential Learning —A CAEL Handbook* (Princeton, N.J.: Educational Testing Service, 1977), pp. v-vii.

11. Nicholas Hobbs, *The Futures of Children* (San Francisco: Jossey-Bass, Inc., 1975), p. 7.

12. K. Patricia Cross, personal communication.

13. For an excellent discussion of individualized education in higher education, see Thomas Clark, "Individualized Education," in *The Modern American College*, ed. A. W. Chickering and associates.

BIBLIOGRAPHY

Adler, Alfred. *Understanding Human Nature*. Cleveland, World Publishing Co., 1927.

Binet, Alfred. *The Development of Intelligence in Children (The Binet-Simon Scale)*. Baltimore: Williams and Wilkins Co., 1916.

Branden, Nathaniel. *The Psychology of Self-Esteem*. Los Angeles: Nash Publishing Corp., 1969.

Bruner, Jerome S. *The Process of Education*. Cambridge, Mass.: Harvard University Press, 1960.

Carnegie Commission on Higher Education. *The Fourth Revolution: Instructional Technology in Higher Education*. New York: McGraw-Hill, 1972.

Chickering, Arthur W. *Education and Identity*. San Francisco: Jossey-Bass, Inc., 1969.

Chickering, Arthur W., and Associates. *The Modern American College*. San Francisco: Jossey-Bass, Inc., 1981.

Chickering, Arthur W., and Chickering, Joanne N. "Lifelong Learning by Handicapped Persons." In *Futures of Education for Exceptional Students: Emerging Structures*, edited by M. C. Reynolds. Minneapolis, Minn.: National Support Systems Project, 1978.

Combs, Arthur W. "Humanizing Education: The Person in the Process." In *Humanizing Education: The Person in the Process*, edited by Robert Leeper. Washington, D.C.: The Association for Supervision and Curriculum Development, 1967.

Combs, Arthur, and Snygg, Donald. *Individualized Behavior: A New Frame of Reference for Psychology*. New York: Harper Bros., 1949.

Dewey, John. *Experience and Education*. New York: Collier Books, 1963.
_____. *Moral Principles in Education*. Boston: Houghton Mifflin, 1909.

Duley, John, and Gordon, Sheila. *College-Sponsored Experiential Learning—A CAEL Handbook*. Princeton, N.J.: Educational Testing Service, 1977.

Erikson, Erik H. *Childhood and Society*. New York: W. W. Norton & Co., 1950.
_____. *Identity and Life Cycle*. New York: International Universities Press, 1969.
_____. *Identity, Youth and Crisis*. New York: W. W. Norton & Co., 1968.

Flavell, John H. *The Developmental Psychology of Jean Piaget*. Princeton, N.J.: D. Van Nostrand Co., 1963.

Freud, Sigmund. *The Basic Writings of Sigmund Freud*. Translated and edited by A. A. Brill. New York: Random House, 1938.

Froebel, Friedrick. *Pedagogics of the Kindergarten*. Translated by Josephine Jarvis. New York: D. Appleton, 1895.

Guilford, Joy P. *The Nature of Intelligence*. New York: McGraw-Hill, 1967.

Gilligan, Carol. *In a Different Voice*. Cambridge, Mass.: Harvard University Press, 1982.

Hobbs, Nicholas. *The Futures of Children*. San Francisco: Jossey-Bass, Inc., 1975.

James, William. *Principles of Psychology*. New York: Henry Holt and Co., 1890.

Jung, Carl Gustav. *The Collected Works of C. G. Jung*. Edited by Herbert Read, Michael Fordham, and Gerhard Adler. New York: Pantheon Books, 1953.

Kelly, George A. *The Psychology of Personal Constructs*. New York: W. W. Norton & Co., 1955.

Klausmeier, Herbert J. *Learning and Human Abilities: Educational Psychology*. New York: Harper Bros., 1961.

Kohlberg, Lawrence. *The Philosophy of Moral Development: Moral Stages and the Idea of Justice*. San Francisco: Harper & Row, 1981.

Loevinger, Jane. *Ego Development: Conceptions and Theories*. San Francisco: Jossey-Bass, Inc., 1976.

Maslow, Abraham H. *Motivation and Personality*. New York: Harper & Row, 1954.

Moustakas, Clark. *Creativity and Conformity*. Princeton, N.J.: D. Van Nostrand Co., 1967.

May, Rollo. *The Courage to Create*. New York: W. W. Norton & Co., 1975.

Newcomb, Theodore M. *Personality and Social Change: Attitude Formation in a Student Community*. New York: Holt, Rinehart & Winston, 1943.

Piaget, Jean. *The Moral Judgment of the Child* (1932). New York: The Free Press, 1965.

Perry, William. *Forms of Intellectual and Ethical Development in the College Years*. New York: Holt, Rinehart & Winston, 1970.

Rogers, Carl R. *Client Centered Therapy*. Boston: Houghton Mifflin, 1951.

_____. *Freedom to Learn: A View of What Education Might Become*. Columbus, Ohio: C. E. Merrill Co., 1969.

_____. *On Becoming a Person: A Therapist's View of Psychotherapy*. Boston: Houghton Mifflin, 1981.

Sanford, Nevitt. "The Developmental Status of the Entering Freshman." In *The American College*, edited by N. Sanford. New York: John Wiley & Sons, 1962.

Skinner, B. F. *Beyond Freedom and Dignity*. New York: Alfred A. Knopf, 1971.

_____. *Science and Human Behavior*. New York: Macmillan, 1953.

Spearman, Charles E. *The Nature of Intelligence and the Principles of Cognition*. London: Macmillan & Co., 1927.

Thurstone, Louis L. *Primary Mental Abilities*. Chicago: University of Chicago Press, 1938.

Watson, John B. *Behavioralism.* New York: W. W. Norton & Co., 1925.

Weathersby, Rita P. "Today's Students and Their Needs." In *The Modern American College*, edited by A. W. Chickering and associates. San Francisco: Jossey-Bass, Inc., 1981.

Weschler, David. *The Measurement of Adult Intelligence*. Baltimore: Williams and Wilkins Co., 1939.

White, Robert W. *Lives in Progress*. New York: Dryden Press, 1958.

Yankelovich, Daniel. *New Rules: Searching for Self-Fulfillment in a World Turned Upside Down*. New York: Random House, 1981.

6

Socialization and Conformity in Education

Gail E. Thomas

> The business of socialization in a formal institutional setting begins for most individuals in the kindergarten class. It proceeds throughout our school experience and hounds us into adult life."
> —Kathryn Borman, 1978

In this chapter, the concepts and role of socialization and conformity as educational goals and practices will be examined. First, these concepts will be defined. In addition, a variety of literature will be reviewed on socialization and conformity as educational goals and practices. The discussion will focus primarily on educational policies and practices concerning socialization and conformity at the elementary and secondary school level rather than at the secondary and post-secondary school levels. The reason for the former focus is that the major part of school socialization and the molding and establishment of students' behavior occurs during the earlier years (i.e., at the kindergarten and elementary school levels) rather than during the junior and senior high school years (Parsons, 1959; Clute, 1976; Borman, 1978). This chapter will also delineate and discuss four features or characteristics of the educational system that are important in educating and socializing students. These features include the school system, the school classroom, school teachers, and school textbooks.

CONCEPTUAL AND HISTORICAL FRAMEWORK RELEVANT TO SCHOOL SOCIALIZATION AND EDUCATIONAL CONFORMITY

The Concepts of Socialization and Conformity

At the most basic level, socialization is the process by which individuals are trained to fit or mesh into social environments, while conformity means action in compliance with customs or in accordance with some given standard of authority. In a broader sense, social scientists have defined socialization as the act or process of teaching children societal norms and providing them with various incentives to accept these norms and behave according to them. More recently, Kazepides (1982) has employed the term socialization to describe the diverse and complex process by which young children, born of different families and with vast potential for different types of behavior, come to adopt the specific language, customs, beliefs, and values of the dominant group. Thus, to a great extent the terms socialization and conformity can be used interchangeably because they both imply compliance to an established set of group norms. Kazepides noted further, however, that socialization or conformity is not an option that is available to some persons and not to others; rather, "it is a necessary condition for growing up as a human being." As a result, one learns to be a participant in the broader society, thereby conforming to the rules and expectation of the dominant group. George Herbert Mead's definition of the self, and Charles H. Cooley's (1958) emphasis on the major role that primary (i.e., family and peers) and secondary groups (i.e., schools and other social institutions) play in nurturing and molding human nature illustrate the profound influence of the socialization process and the agents of socialization. As Mead noted: "The self is something which has a development; it is not initially there at birth, but arises in the process of social experience and activity; that is, it develops in the given individual as a result of his relations to that process as a whole and to other individuals within that process (Mead, 1934: 135).

Children's definition of the self and social reality begins with the family (the primary agency of socialization) and continues throughout their schooling and through interaction in other social institutions. Like the family, the school is an institution that represents the adult authority figure in society. However, unlike the family, the school is a more formal system with established rules and regulations. Because the school is both a reflection and extension of the larger society it cannot expect to substantially deviate from the ideas, norms, and values of society. In fact, it has been argued that schools function to reinforce and preserve the status quo (Havinghurst and Neugarten, 1976; Thayer and Levit, 1969; Persell, 1977; Carnoy, 1972). Thus, the purpose of schooling must necessarily be defined beyond its curriculum offerings and its cognitive dimensions.

Historical Context

In the nineteenth and early twentieth centuries, education for conformity and socialization was consistent with the original intent of American education (Thayer and Levit, 1969). During this time, American education emphasized social cohesion, conformity, and authority. The entrance of a substantial number of new immigrants to the United States and the threat of a variety of new subcultures were major factors that reinforced the American tradition of education for conformity and socialization. American schools assumed the role of a "melting pot" for new entrants into American life. In describing the situation, Thayer and Levit noted that "for the children of the newly enfranchised as well as for the children of immigrants, American public schools exercised a molding influence that was essentially conservative in character." The authors further noted that the schools functioned during this time to transmit American culture, and to assimilate the children of immigrants rather than to welcome new subcultures and the new patterns of living that these immigrants offered.

The relationship between schooling and American identity was clearly and securely formulated by the end of the nineteenth century. At this time, major concern was expressed in establishing a "unified nation." As a result, American schools became a focus for patriotism where students learned how to become "good" citizens. During this period, textbooks were to be memorized and recited in class. These books were to reveal the school's expectations about society's cultural values. Also the importance of good conduct and having values that conformed to American society were emphasized in these texts. For example, Lazerson noted that *McGuffey's Reader* was the most popular American school textbook during the nineteenth century. The text, which was by William Holmes McGuffey, sold over 120 million copies between 1836 and 1920. The content of the text reflected morals for good conduct, middle-class values, and the importance of the American work ethic. The following passage from the text illustrates the latter point: "Work, work my boy, be not afraid; look labor boldly in the face; take up the hammer and the spade; and blush not for your humble place." This passage conveyed to students that getting ahead involved allegiance to the American Protestant work ethic, and that hard work and frugality brought prosperity. Other themes and important American messages that the text conveyed were: (1) responsibility and success or failure lay with the individual; (2) the affluent should use their wealth in socially responsible ways; (3) disobedience was unconscionable; (4) persistence, punctuality, honesty, self-denial, and temperance defined the moral man; (5) individuals should accept the fact that they live in a hierarchical society (Lazerson, 1978).

Theories of Educational Socialization and Conformity

Three major theories are frequently relied upon as a basis for understanding school socialization: structural-functional theory, phenomenological theory, and neo-Marxist theory. The structural-functional theory argues that all social institutions, social arrangements, and patterns of social stratification in society function for the good and welfare of society and the individual (Davis and Moore, 1945; Durkheim, 1956). However, the group's interest and the maintenance of group cohesion and social equilibrium are held to be more important than the individual's interests. Thus, cooperation and consensus are critical elements of this theoretical framework. The functionalist perspective also views social stratification within schools and within other social institutions as inevitable. Such stratification is viewed by functionalists as solely the result of individual ability and effort.

In terms of the school system, the structural-functional paradigm emphasizes how schools socialize students to accept rather than to challenge the norms and mores of the larger society. According to the functionalist perspective, the schools provide a valuable service in training students to uphold social commitments and to learn the cognitive and social skills required by society (Parsons, 1959; Dreeben, 1968). Emile Durkheim captured the essence of the functionalist perspective as it relates to schooling by posing the following question: "Of what use is it to imagine a kind of education that would be fatal to the society that put it into practice?" In responding to this question Durkheim noted that "citizens ... therefore must be methodically socialized (taught, *indoctrinated*, conditioned, trained, constrained, etc.) to acquire those attributes that will guarantee the survival of society" (Durkheim, 1956).

The second theoretical perspective that has been applied to the goals and function of schools is the phenomenological perspective (Giroux and Penna, 1979). According to this perspective, any valid theory of school socialization (or socialization in general) must be viewed as a theory of the construction of social reality in which meaning is made interactively between the agent(s) of socialization and the individual(s) being socialized (O'Neill, 1973). This view also holds that students are more active than passive in the learning and socialization process; and that socialization is a bilateral rather than a unilateral process. Proponents of the phenomenological approach hold that this perspective provides a more complete description of what actually occurs during socialization. It is also considered unique because it attributes importance to the student in defining and redefining reality, and in influencing as well as being influenced by the schools and by school officials. It is at the same time more dynamic and more subtle, changing the social reality of the individual.

The third theoretical perspective, the neo-Marxian perspective is similar to the functionalist perspective in that it is a macro- rather than a micro-level theory that also acknowledges the integral relationship between the goals and the stratification system of schools and the broader society. However, unlike the functionalist perspective, proponents of the neo-Marxian perspective contend that schools are agents of socialization that function to preserve the status quo and the values of the dominant group (Carnoy, 1972; Bowles and Gintis, 1976; Persell, 1977).

The neo-Marxist perspective also views group conflict and competition rather than consensus and cooperation as the central element or characteristic of group interaction. Lazerson's historical account of American education acknowledges the role and reality of conflict between ethnic minorities and the dominant group in U. S. society. He noted that during the nineteenth and twentieth centuries ethnic groups and new immigrants were constantly at odds with political and educational authorities concerning the teaching of alternative cultural values and languages. In instances where immigrant groups possessed sufficient political power, foreign languages (especially German and French) were included in elementary and secondary school curricula.

Also throughout most of the nineteenth century, blacks were excluded from American efforts to create a "melting pot" or homogeneous culture. Lazerson noted that "race was the line that could not be crossed in the melting pot of the common school." In response, blacks actively protested this exclusion. Their response varied from the establishment of their own separate schools (with the assistance of northern missionaries) to efforts to integrate the schools from which they were originally excluded. Thus, racial and ethnic conflict concerning the goals and purpose of education has historically been and presently remains an important feature of American education. The "search for excellence" remains in conflict with the goal of equity and adequacy for minority students. In addition, evidence that will be presented later in this chapter will show that the extent to which schools should educate versus socialize students also constitutes an ongoing debate in American education.

Reinforcement Theory

Reinforcement theory is a fourth theory of importance in understanding the manner in which schools socialize students and elicit performance, support, and cooperation from members (i.e., teachers, counselors, and support staff). Like the phenomenological perspective, reinforcement theory is primarily a social psychological theory that is more applicable at the micro (i.e., student and classroom) than at the macro (i.e., societal or broader institutional) level. The primary thesis of reinforcement theory is that individuals are motivated to act or behave in various prescribed or desired ways through the institution and application of various types of rewards and punishments that serve as powerful reinforcement incentives (Festinger, 1964).

Teacher praise and sanctions are reinforcement incentives that influence students' behavior. However, school grades are the most important reinforcers that are employed by teachers and by school systems to reinforce (either negatively or positively) and assess student behavior. Grades are extremely important in that they are the primary method by which students prove their worth. Grades also determine students' promotion from year to year, and whether they remain in school, graduate and/or enter college. In addition, they have a critical influence on students' self-esteem, and influence the perceptions that "significant others" (i.e., parents, peers) have of students and their ability (Harrison, 1976). However, as Dreeben noted, teachers must initially establish grades as sanctions so that students will regard high grades as rewarding and low grades as punishing (Dreeben, 1968). Harrison noted that by the time that most students enter high school and college they are well socialized regarding the importance of grades. As a result, students who accept the system are likely to conform to rather than deviate from their teachers' instructions and expectations based on their desire to receive good grades.

AGENTS OF SOCIALIZATION AND
THEIR MODE OF INFLUENCE

The School System

The school system in general has been viewed as a sorting and selection agency that trains and socializes individuals for different educational and occupational attainments (Havinghurst and Neugarten, 1976;

Thayer and Levit, 1969; Persell, 1977; Bowles and Gintis, 1976). Bowles and Gintis have described the situation as follows: "The differential socialization patterns in schools attended by students of different social classes, even within the same schools, do not arise by accident. Rather, they stem from the fact that the educational objectives and expectations of administrators, teachers, and parents, and the responsiveness of students to various patterns of teaching and control differ for students of different social classes" (1976: 77-87).

Studies have also shown that various practices and structural arrangements of the school (i.e., tracking, curriculum materials including textbooks) contribute to differential and traditional race and sex socialization (Sells, 1976; Nilsen, 1977; Persell, 1977; Ayim, 1979). Two general approaches may be employed by schools in differentially socializing students (Hamilton, 1983). A school may consciously and overtly specify the tasks of socializing students. In doing so, school officials will disseminate public documents that have explicit statements concerning this goal and the values and subject content to be included in school curricula and transmitted to students. Teachers are often held accountable for their success or lack of success in transmitting these values and goals to students. Traditional and modern perennialists (Hutchins, Adler, Barr) support such an approach. Alternatively, a school system may choose to consciously or unconsciously transmit the values and goals of socialization to students without making this information available to the public. This latter approach is often referred to as the "hidden curriculum" (Giroux and Penna, 1979; Hamilton, 1983). Hamilton contends that this second approach is more powerful and potentially threatening because it cannot be readily or easily scrutinized by the general public.

The School Class as a System of Socialization

In a 1959 article entitled, "The School Class as a Social System," Talcott Parsons described the elementary and secondary school class as an agency of socialization and allocation. Parsons argued that while the school class is a small unit in the school system and in the larger society, it is the central place and mechanism where the "business of formal education and socialization for subsequent educational and occupational roles occurs."

According to Parsons, the main process of differentiation in elementary and secondary school classes occurs in curriculum placement (i.e., the sorting of students into college-bound vs. non-college-bound tracks). In addition, he noted that the sorting and selection of students into various academic tracks *begins* at the elementary school level and is well established before students complete junior high school. Thus students' track placement at this point is viewed by Parsons as a good determinant of their subsequent track assignment. Parsons also noted that students' track assignment and classroom evaluation are based on ascriptive (i.e., social class, sex, race) factors as well as on merit.

In a 1983 study of the structural arrangement and socialization features of the school class, Hamilton identified three concepts that are operative at the level of classroom socialization. The first concept refers to the group structure of school classes and the fact that in most traditional schools, student learning occurs within groups (especially at the elementary and junior high school levels). As a result of having to function in groups, students are constantly confronted with delays in getting the teacher's attention. While students' personal need for recognition is subordinated, they do learn *order* and *conformity* in this process. Students also learn to function within the context of a group.

The second concept that Hamilton referred to is praise. Both praise and disapproval are constantly given to students by teachers and their peers. Through the process of being sanctioned and evaluated publicly, students learn to handle stress and to balance their teacher evaluations and expectations with the expectations of their peers. Recent gender research has demonstrated that differential treatment by parents and teachers results in different self-expectations and patterns of socialization within the classroom (Gilligan, 1982). Power is the third concept that Hamilton identified. He noted that power is constantly being exercised in the classroom by teachers. Also, while students experience and learn about the concept of power from adult authorities in their families, they encounter a more impersonal type of power from the teacher. This power is more akin to the power that operates in the larger society. Thus, through exposure and interaction with teachers and with classroom power and authority structures, students learn to respect and conform to authority figures and authority structures in society. Power situations in the classroom in seating, teacher attitudes, and peer relationships have an impact upon minorities and women. The conflict between expectations of conformity and the impetus for individual creativity continues to be unresolved in modern classrooms.

Teachers as Agents of School Socialization

Despite the many constraints that teachers are confronted with, they continue to define the moral order and style of learning and socialization that takes place in the school classroom (Borman, 1978). However, teachers must always win the respect of students and daily negotiate their control over students. In gaining control in the classroom and creating a basis for student respect and conformity, most traditional teachers have employed authoritarian and disciplinarian type approaches to student learning and socialization (Walsh and Cowles, 1979). These techniques are based on punitive sanctions that are used by teachers to elicit appropriate student behavior. Also, learning based on this traditional model primarily involves unilateral communication from teacher to student.

Recently, more nontraditional and innovative learning and socialization techniques have been employed by American schoolteachers (Walsh and Cowles, 1979). These techniques entail bilateral communication and interaction between teachers and students. Research has shown that these approaches along with systematic teacher training have a more positive influence on student conduct and learning than the use of punitive and authoritarian methods (Hyman, 1977; Grant, 1979).

More democratic teaching and leadership styles have emerged among classroom teachers since the latter half of the 1960s when the general public and various authors (Kozol, 1967; Kohl, 1968; Silberman, 1970) began to challenge the authoritarian structures of American schools. These individuals advocated students' rights, and the need for more humanism and democracy in the schools.

However, despite differences in teaching and leadership styles (i.e., traditional vs. nontraditional) most teachers in American public schools perceive and treat students as members of groups rather than as distinct individuals (Borman, 1978). Teachers have also been found to hold different expectations and perceptions of students based on their academic ability and their ascriptive attributes (Rosenthal, 1973; Jackson, 1968; Grant, 1979).

Apart from the limited literature on teacher authority and teacher expectations, very little is known about the specific nature of teacher socialization and its impact on students. Grant noted that a better understanding of school, classroom, and teacher socialization might be gained by recognizing and examining more closely the reciprocal nature of the socialization process between students and teachers, and between students and school administrators. Also, the nature and impact of student-peer relations on classroom and student-teacher interaction and socialization may be an important contingency. Coleman and others (Waller, 1961; Cusick, 1973), for example, have documented the existence of a strong peer culture among students in junior and senior high school. This subculture is often in conflict or in opposition to the goals and values and authority structure of the schools and school classrooms (Coleman, 1961). Thus additional studies on the influence of peer culture on student learning and socialization are needed.

Finally, the extent to which the present decline in the morale and quality of the teaching profession (The National Commission on Excellence in Education, 1983), the increase in school decentralization, and the decrease in teacher authority (Metz, 1978) influence the ability of school administrators and teachers to socialize students and to obtain student cooperation and conformity needs to be examined. Metz noted that schools have lost many of their traditional resources for controlling students which include these factors. Also, state laws, court decisions, and community groups and parents have recently not only challenged schools but have been successful in limiting the authority of schools. Conformity and traditional values are characteristic of community pressure. Metz also noted that because of grade inflation and the fact that grades are only important incentives for highly motivated students, they have lost their value and utility as tools for teacher control.

School Textbooks as Tools of School Socialization

While less prevalent and influential than *McGuffey's Readers* in 1836, school textbooks are at present important tools for school socialization. Recently, a number of criticisms have been made regarding the content of elementary and secondary school social studies textbooks (Apple, 1971; Ayon, 1978; Fox and Hess, 1972). For example, Fox and Hess noted that what schools consider objective knowledge in social studies textbooks is often a biased portrayal of American society that ignores political and other forms of social conflict. In their study of fifty-eight social studies textbooks drawn from a sample of textbooks adopted by eight states in the United States for students in the third, fifth, and ninth grades, Fox and Hess found that the American political system was described as if it were overwhelmingly consensual. The authors further stated that "people in the textbooks were pictured as easily getting together discussing their differences and rationally arriving at decision." Moreover, everyone in the text was recorded as having accepted the decisions at hand.

Ayon noted that the unrealistic and overtly positive nature of school textbooks is not a reflection of poor critical thinking on the part of schools, but rather inherent in the general process of school socialization. Ayon further noted that the school social studies textbooks that are consciously selected by school administrators function to foster student conformity and acceptance of the legitimacy of existing social institutions.

Giroux and Penna (1979) reported that in addition to the overt and covert messages that are portrayed by school textbooks, the manner in which social studies knowledge and other educational materials are selected and presented to students reflects a priori assumptions by teachers and school administrators about the value and legitimacy of these materials. Furthermore, the ideological choices and considerations that schools impose in selecting teaching and curriculum materials structure students' perception of the world and of what institutional arrangements and values are or are not legitimate. The conscious and profound effect of this process has been summarized by Berger and Luckmann as follows: "All institutions, by the very fact of their existence, control human conduct by setting up predefined patterns of conduct, which channel human behavior in one direction as against the many other directions that would theoretically be possible. It is important to stress that this controlling character is inherent in institutionalization" (1967: 55).

CONCLUSION

The literature and educational theories reviewed in this chapter clearly indicate that conformity and educational socialization are integral and major aspects of American school programs and school curricula and that educational socialization is a multilevel process that takes place in the school, classroom, and throughout all instructional and curriculum levels. In addition, the evidence shows that traditional and earlier forms of student socialization by the schools entailed a more unilateral and authoritarian approach, while more recent and nontraditional methods of socialization have involved a bilateral process of interaction in which student and teacher socialization is reciprocal.

The literature also shows that while educational socialization functions in part to prepare students for adult roles, it also serves to differentially socialize and stratify students and occupational statuses. Thus, apart from merit as a basis for educating and socializing students, ascription still remains an important factor of selection in American school systems.

The evidence presented in this chapter indicates that race, sex, and social-class bias in the socialization and educational process work to the disadvantage of women, low-income students, and various ethnic and racial minorities (i.e., blacks, Hispanics, and native Americans). Recent studies show that independent of their ability, these groups have achieved and continue to achieve a lower level and quality of educational and occupational attainment (Alexander and Eckland, 1974; Mednick, Tangri, and Hoffman, 1975; Alvarez, 1979; Morris, 1979; Thomas and Hargett, 1981). These studies have in part attributed the lower attainment levels and quality of attainment of women and disadvantaged minorities to early educational tracking practices, and differences in traditional race, sex, and class socialization.

Several proposals have been advocated, and in some cases implemented, in an attempt to alter traditional race and sex socialization, and to increase student choice. Ethnic studies programs and curriculum materials have been incorporated in public schools on a national basis. The open education and the free school movements in the late 1960s were efforts designed to replace traditional, authoritarian educational structures with more liberal and democratic ones that were ideographic rather than conformist (Kozol, 1967; Kohl, 1968; Silberman, 1970).

In characterizing the trends in American education, one could argue that the authoritarian and education-for-conformity models in the nineteenth and early twentieth centuries represented a "pendulum swing in American education" to the extreme right, while the open education and free school movements in the late 1960s represented a drastic swing back to the left. The more recent "back-to-basics" movement represents a return of the pendulum in American education back to the right. The potential impact of this latter movement and the extent to which Americans will remain comfortable with it is at present uncertain. What is certain is that irrespective of the theme or climate of American education, education for socialization and conformity will continue to be a part of the goals and curricula of American education. The debate as to which of these two goals should receive the greatest priority will continue as a subject of controversy among Americans into the unforeseeable future.

REFERENCES

Alexander, Karl L., and Eckland, Bruce K. 1974. "Sex Differences in the Educational Attainment Process." *American Sociological Review* 5: 668-81.
Alvarez, R., and Lutterman, K. G. 1979. *Discrimination in Organizations.* San Francisco: Jossey-Bass, Inc.
Apple, Michael W. 1971. "Curriculum as Ideological Selection." *Comparative Education Review* 20 (June): 210-11.

Ayim, Maryann E. 1979. "What Price Socialization? From the Ledgers of the Oppressed." *Interchange* 10: 78-94.

Ayon, Jean. 1978. "Elementary Social Studies Textbook and Legitimating Knowledge." *Theory and Research in Social Education* 6: 40-54.

Berger, Peter L., and Luchmann, Thomas. 1967. *The Social Construction of Reality: A Treatise in the Sociology of Knowledge.* New York: Doubleday.

Borman, Kathryn. 1978. "Social Control and the Process of Schooling: A Study of Socialization of Kindergarten Children in Two Settings." *Urban Education* 13: 295-322.

Bowles, Samuel, and Gintis, Herbert. 1976. *Schooling in Capitalistic America.* New York: Basic Books.

Brodinsky, Ben. 1977. "Back to the Basics: The Movement and its Meaning." *Phi Delta Kappan* 58: 522-27.

Carnoy, Martin. 1972. *Schooling in a Corporate Society.* New York: David McKay.

Clute, Marrel P. 1976. "Can Human Rights Survive the Classroom?" In *Challenge and Choice in Contemporary Education*, edited by Christopher J. Lucas, New York: Macmillan.

Coleman, James. 1961. *The Adolescent Society.* New York: The Free Press.

Cooley, Charles H. 1958. *Social Organization.* New York: The Free Press.

Cusick, P. 1973. *Inside High School.* New York: Holt, Rinehart & Winston.

Davis, Kingsley, and Moore, Wilbert E. 1945. "Some Principles of Stratification." *American Sociological Review* 10: 242-49.

Dreeben, Robert. 1968. *On What is Learned in School.* Philippines: Addison Wesley Publishers.

Durkheim, Emile. 1956. *Education and Sociology.* New York: The Free Press.

Festinger, L. 1964. "Motivation Leading to Social Behavior." In *Nebraska Symposium on Motivation*, edited by M. R. Jones, pp. 191-219. Lincoln: University of Nebraska Press.

Fox, Thomas E., and Hess, Robert D. 1972. *An Analysis of Social Conflict in Social Studies Textbooks.* Washington, D.C.: Government Printing Office.

Gilligan, Carol. 1982. *In a Different Voice. Psychological Theory and Women's Development.* Cambridge, Mass.: Harvard University Press.

Giroux, Henry, and Penna, Anthony N. 1979. "Social Education in the Classroom: The Dynamics of the Hidden Curriculum." *Theory and Research in Social Education* 7: 21-43.

Grant, Carl A. 1979. "Classroom Socialization: The Other Side of a Two-Way Street." *Educational Leadership* 36: 470-74.

Hamilton, Stephen F. 1983. "Synthesizing of Research on the Social Side of Schooling." *Educational Leadership* 40: 65-72.

Harrison, Alton. 1976. "Humanism and Educational Reform." In *Challenge and Choice in Contemporary Education*, edited by Christopher J. Lucas, pp. 212-18. New York: Macmillan.

Havinghurst, Robert J., and Neugarten, Bernice L. 1976. *Society and Education.* Boston: Allyn and Bacon.

Hyman, Irwin A. 1979. "Discipline in American Education." *Journal of Education* 161: 51-70.

Jackson, Philip. 1968. *Life in Classrooms.* New York: Holt, Rinehart & Winston.

Kazepides, Tasos. 1982. "Educating, Socializing, and Indoctrinating." *Journal of Philosophy of Education* 16: 155-65.

Kohl, Herbert. 1968. *Children.* New York: Signet.

Kozol, Jonathan. 1967. *Death at an Early Age.* Boston: Houghton Mifflin.

Lazerson, Marvin. 1978. "The School as a Melting Pot: Pluralism and Americanization Vie for Dominance." *Civil Rights Digest* 11: 18-27.

McNelly, Geraldine. 1981. *Child Socialization and Education: Innovative Open Education: Its Goals and Values.* ERIC-ED 177026. Syracuse, N.Y.: ERIC Clearinghouse, Syracuse University.

Mead, George Herbert. 1934. *Mind, Self and Society.* Chicago: University of Chicago Press.

Mednick, M. T., Tangri, S. S., and Hoffman, L. W. 1975. *Women and Achievement.* New York: John Wiley & Sons.

Metz, Mary H. 1978. "Clashes in the Classroom: The Importance of Norms of Authority." *Education and Urban Society* 11: 13-19.

Morris, Lorenzo. 1979. *Elusive Equality: The Status of Black Americans in Higher Education.* Washington, D.C.: Howard University Press.

National Commission on Excellence in Education. 1983. *A Nation at Risk.* Washington, D.C.: Government Printing Office.

Nilsin, A. P. 1977. "Sexism in Children's Books and Elementary Teaching Materials." *Sexism and Language.* Urbana, Ill.: National Council of Teaching English.

O'Neill, John. 1973. "Embodiment and Child Development: A Phenomenological Approach." In *Childhood and Socialization*, edited by Hans Peter Dreitzel, pp. 65-81. New York: Macmillan.

Parsons, Talcott. 1959. "The School Class as a Social System: Some of Its Functions in American Society." *Harvard Educational Review* 29: 297-318.

Persell, Caroline Hodges. 1977. *Education and Inequality.* New York: The Free Press.

Rosenbaum, J. E. 1976. *Making Inequality.* New York: John Wiley & Sons.

Rosenthal, Robert. 1973. "The Pygmalion Effect Lives." *Psychology Today* 7: 56-58.

Sells, Lucy. 1976. "The Mathematics Filter and the Education of Women and Minorities." Paper presented at the annual meeting of the American Association for the Advancement of Science, Boston, Massachusetts.

Silberman, Charles E. 1970. *Crisis in the Classroom: The Remaking of American Education.* New York: Random House.

Thayer, V. T., and Levitz, Martin. 1969. *The Roles of the School in American Education.* New York: Dodd Mead.

Thomas, Gail E., and Hargett, Stella L. 1983. "Socialization Effects and Black College Female Educational and Occupational Orientation." *Journal of Social and Behavioral Sciences* 10: 18-27.

Tyack, David B. 1967. *Turning Points in American Education.* Waltham, Mass.: Blaisdell.

Waller, W. 1961. *The Sociology of Teaching.* New York: John Wiley & Sons.

Walsh, Kevin, and Cowles, Milly. 1979. "Social Consciousness and Disciplines in the Urban Elementary School." *The Urban Review* 11: 25-32.

PART FOUR

CONCLUSION

7

Who Shall Be Educated?

Charles V. Willie and Inabeth Miller

It has often been stated that the role of the federal government in education is a minor and limited one, that public education in this nation is a state and local responsibility. This assertion is made largely because the financial contribution of the federal government to public education is relatively small and public education is not specifically mentioned as a federal responsibility in the Constitution.

Based on the data presented in this study, we arrive at a different conclusion. The role of the federal government is fundamental, not in financing the availability of education but in fashioning and enforcing principles that guarantee equal access to it.

Some levels of government are capable of handling some functions better than other levels. Equity educational issues involving the distribution of common resources in a way that is fair are appropriately handled at the local level, when all local constituents are eligible to participate directly or through representatives in the decision-making process. These kinds of issues are appropriately local because there seldom is a single solution that is always the best solution. When the practicalities of the situation are considered, the participants make appropriate compromises and trade-offs which is the usual way that negotiated decisions are reached.

Issues of educational access, however, have to do with the fashioning of principles and guidelines regarding who shall be educated. Matters of principle are most appropriately handled at a level of government that is distant from local pressures and prejudices. Because the Constitution of the United States is the ultimate guarantor of the rights of individuals, the federal government is the appropriate level to handle issues of equality of access.

The record shows that the federal government followed a hands-off policy the first half of the twentieth century regarding the matter of equal access in education. The hands-off policy was more or less a result of the *Plessy* Supreme Court decision of 1896 that legalized "separate but equal" treatment for blacks and other ethnic minorities. Although the federal government sanctioned segregation, it was obligated by law to guarantee that the segregated public education blacks and ethnic minorities received was equal to that offered to whites. This the federal government did not do; and the nation reaped a whirlwind of enraged minorities who demonstrated in public squares and disrupted the public order to secure their rights. When the federal government finally assumed its responsibility to guarantee equal access to education after the 1954 *Brown* Supreme Court decision, the Civil Rights Act of 1964, and the Voting Rights Act of 1965, public order returned to our local communities.

One could hypothesize that segregated education would have ended in the United States many years earlier if the federal government had assumed its responsibility of fashioning and enforcing the principle of equality of access. Although segregation was sanctioned by law the first half of this century, separate educational opportunities were required to be equal for all races. The federal government by way of its hands-off policy permitted segregation but did not enforce this principle of equality that the Supreme Court had required in the *Plessy* decision. If the equality principle had been enforced, the enormous expense of separate but equal schools would have ended segregation before the 1950s.

With hindsight of what happens to the social fabric of a nation when one level of government defaults on responsibilities that are uniquely its own, the federal government now is taking an active role in fashioning principles pertaining to equality of access for various population groups such as the handicapped who wish to be accommodated in mainstream educational activities, students for whom English is not their first language, and women who want to participate in all educational opportunities, including athletics. Timely legislation enacted by Congress has established firm guidelines and principles for redressing the grievances of these population groups so that they are not required to disrupt the public order to obtain their rights as blacks and others had done earlier.

Even the equity issues that are best handled at the local level could not be dealt with effectively when the local policy-making groups were homogeneous, consisting of representatives of only one racial group.

These homogeneous, decision-making bodies in local governments resulted from at-large elections. They violated the "one person, one vote" principle. But localities were reluctant to conform to this principle until the federal government enforced it by requiring them to elect policymakers by districts rather than at large. Local elections by single-member districts have resulted in greater diversity in the membership of school boards and consequently more equitable decision making.

Clearly, the federal government has played a fundamental role in public education in fashioning and enforcing principles pertaining to equality of access. Had the federal government not assumed this responsibility, segregation of all sorts and conditions of people would have continued as the norm and many local communities probably would have fractionated into warring racial and ethnic groups.

The increased responsibility for guaranteeing equal access to educational opportunities that the federal government assumed during the latter half of the twentieth century probably helped the nation achieve universal education at elementary and secondary levels. Universal education has been a goal for which the nation has striven over several decades. This goal is reflected in the compulsory school attendance laws enacted by the states. Beginning in the 1980s, universal education was nearly achieved with more than 90 percent of all school-age children enrolled in school.

We conclude that the civil rights movement assisted the nation in achieving this goal. Some evidence that appears to support this conclusion is the dramatic reduction since the 1940s in the difference between majority and minority populations in the level of education achieved. During the age of officially sanctioned segregation, a difference of more than 50 percent separated blacks and whites in the median year of schooling that each group received. After the *Brown* v. *Board of Education* Supreme Court decision and the Civil Rights Act of 1964, and public laws pertaining to education of the handicapped and foreign-language groups, the difference between the races in median school year attained began to decrease and reached a small difference of less than 1 percent as the 1980s began.

The nation has now achieved a consensus about who shall be educated. It has decided forthrightly that all sorts and conditions of people should be admitted to public schools. But the nation is seriously divided on what these specific population groups should learn. In high school, for example, is there a common core of information that all students should know? Should the subject matter taught differ for students who plan to enter the labor force immediately after high school graduation and those who plan to go on to college or some other form of postsecondary education? Should students be taught in groups that are more or less homogeneous in aptitude, or is there mutual advantage for instruction in heterogenous classes? What is the responsibility of the schools for fostering music and art appreciation and competence to perform in these fields? Is the attainment of physical fitness appropriately or inappropriately labeled as education? Should students who are not facile in the use of the English language be taught in their native language in school? The chapters prepared for this volume indicate a lack of consensus on these and other matters as we move toward the end of the twentieth century. Some of these issues have been debated for more than one hundred years.

A tentative consensus appears to be emerging around the concept of a comprehensive school. But agreement breaks down with each attempt to operationally define the specific components of a comprehensive education. The series of reports on educational reform reveal the continuing absence of a common opinion about what is basic and essential in education.

We conclude, based on the information contained in this book, that a consensus on the essential components of a comprehensive education has eluded us during the course of this century because we have not yet as a nation come to a common understanding about the purpose of education. With a clearer understanding of the purpose of education, the nation could resolve some of the contradictions in the approaches to education proposed in various educational reform reports.

An examination of purpose should focus not on the nation as if it had a single norm but on the various population groups and their multiple norms. Within any national collectivity there are at least two sets of norms—those of the dominant people of power and those of the subdominant people of power.

From the beginning of this century, the purpose of education, from the perspective of the dominant people of power, has been to instill a common culture in all of the people. To fulfill this goal, schools were expected to function as carriers of culture rather than as critics of it.

The Americanization movement during the 1920s for immigrant populations is a good example of the school functioning as an institution of social control, helping newcomers to conform to the customs of the dominant people of power. This approach to education was fostered as a way of unifying the country. And schools were expected to serve the interests and needs of other institutions. For example, schools were expected to prepare students for successful entry into the labor force and to indoctrinate young citizens with a sense of citizenship and loyalty to the government. In summary, education from the perspective of the dominant people of power was for the purpose of advancing society.

The subdominant people of power, including racial and ethnic minorities, looked to the public schools to fulfill a different purpose during the early years of this century. They pursued education for the purpose of uplifting and enhancing the individual. By way of education, racial and ethnic minorities sought personal liberation. After the Civil War, many racial minorities were eager to learn to read. Some, especially older blacks, wanted to learn how to read so that they could read the Bible before they died. Others, younger people in particular, believed that education would enhance their opportunities in the work force.

The dominant people of power, also realizing the personal liberating effects of education, established laws prohibiting the teaching of slaves to read and write during the nineteenth century. They continued such discrimination during the first half of the twentieth century. Although blacks and other ethnic minorities were not legally proscribed from learning how to read, their education was substantially different from that which whites received in public schools and was grossly inadequate at the turn of the century. Thus, during the second quarter of the twentieth century, blacks adopted the educational perspective of the dominant people of power as their own and began to challenge local communities to provide a common education for them that was similar to the one provided whites.

Interestingly, after blacks won their demand for a common education and a unitary community school system in the *Brown* decision of 1954, whites during the second half of the twentieth century adopted as their own the orientation toward education that blacks had previously manifested. They looked to education as a means of personal advancement and were less concerned with it as a community-building enterprise. Indeed, the proliferation of private academies and the recurring proposal for education paid for by vouchers issued by public authorities to individuals was seen by some, especially minorities, as a threat to the vitality and welfare of the common public school movement which the dominant people of power had embraced earlier.

It would appear that whites have adopted the orientation toward education that once was normative for blacks and that blacks have adopted the orientation toward education that once was normative for whites. Since dominant and subdominant groups have acknowledged similar purposes for education, although at different times, with one group emphasizing the community advancement theme the first half of this century and the other group emphasizing it during the second half; and since these two groups also acknowledge individual enhancement as an important purpose of education—again the dominants emphasizing it during one period and the subdominants, another—we conclude that both purposes are significant and that one purpose without the other is incomplete. One comes to this conclusion after recognizing that there are always at least two norms in social organization, one articulated by the dominant people of power, and the other by the subdominant people of power, and that both norms are valid and therefore are complementary.

All of this is to say that we may find our way out of the morass of apparent contradictions if we analyze the validity of educational reform proposals from the perspective of the theory of complementarity. According to this theory, the interests of whites (or dominants) and blacks and other ethnic minorities (or subdominants) are not the same. But they can be complementary. Moreover, the interests that subdominants once emphasized may become of value to dominants and vice versa. For this reason, population-specific approaches in educational reform are needed so that the necessarily different interests and needs of different groups may be accommodated. The incentive for following this approach in educational reform is the recognition that one day the interests and concerns of another group may be the interests and concerns of one's own group. Thus, the interests and concerns of both dominants and subdominants exist simultaneously. Both deserve to be cultivated.

Index

About the Editors
and Contributors

ARTHUR W. CHICKERING is Distinguished Professor of Higher Education and Director of the Center for the Study of Higher Education at Memphis State University. After receiving a B.A. degree in modern comparative literature from Wesleyan University (1950) and a M.A. in teaching English from the Graduate School of Education, Harvard University (1951), Chickering completed a Ph.D. degree in school psychology at Teachers College, Columbia University (1958). Presently his is Distinguished Professor and Director of the Center for the Study of Higher Education at Memphis State University.

Chickering is the recipient of the Outstanding Service Award from the National Association of Student Personnel Administrators, a Distinguished Service Citation from the Sex Information and Education Council of the United States, and the Distinguished Contribution to Knowledge Award of the American College Personnel Association. He received the 1985 Lindquist Award from the American Educational Research Association for exceptional contributions to research on college environments, student development, and educational practices in colleges and universities.

Chickering's major publications include *Education and Identity*, which received the 1969 American Council on Education Book Award for its "outstanding contribution to higher education"; *Commuting Versus Resident Students* (1974); *Experience and Learning* (1977); and *Developing the College Curriculum* (with W. Bergquist, D. Halliburton, and J. Lindquist, 1977). He edited *The Modern American College* (1981), a major volume addressing human development and higher education. In addition, he is author of numerous journal articles concerning relationships among educational practices, college environments, and student development.

RICK GINSBERG, Ph.D., is an associate professor in the Department of Educational Leadership and Policies at the University of South Carolina, Columbia, South Carolina. His areas of research interest include the reform process in schools and the politics and history of education. He currently serves as secretary of the Politics of Education Association. Dr. Ginsberg did his doctoral work in administrative, institutional, and policy studies in education at the University of Chicago.

MICHAEL K. GRADY is the research associate with the Magnet Review Committee (MRC) in St. Louis. The committee plans and evaluates magnet schools and reports its findings to the federal district court overseeing the school desegregation case of *Liddell* v. *Board of Education.* Recently, the MRC assisted a court-appointed panel of experts in the development of a long-range plan for the St. Louis magnet schools. Prior to his work with MRC, Mr. Grady consulted with a number of court-appointed monitoring committees in the St. Louis case. In 1984-85, he assisted Charles V. Willie in one such effort, resulting in the publication of *Metropolitan School Desegregation: A Case Study of the St. Louis Voluntary Transfer Program.* Mr. Grady is completing doctoral studies at the Harvard Graduate School of Education in the area of educational research and policy analysis.

ANN Q. LYNCH, Ed.D., is an associate professor in the Counseling and Personnel Services Department of the Center for the Study of Higher Education, Memphis State University. After receiving her B.A. degree from the Duke University (1953) in mathematics and education, Lynch taught high school mathematics in Jacksonville, Florida. She completed her M.Ed. degree in counseling and guidance at the University of Florida (1965) and served as a high school counselor. In 1968 she completed her Ed.D. degree in personnel services at the University of Florida.

Lynch began her career in higher education as a counseling psychologist with the Student Mental Health Service at the University of Florida where she counseled students, supervised trainees, and consulted with campus and community agencies. She codirected National Institute of Mental Health (NIMH) projects on marriage and college life and on training campus community mental health program directors and served on the Preventive Action in College Mental Health Project. She moved to Memphis State University to become executive director of the Higher Education for Adult Mental Health Project (NIMH).

Currently, she teaches marriage and family counseling and consultation courses, coordinates the Center Associates Network, and conducts professional development programs for administrators, faculty, and student services professionals. She is a licensed psychologist and serves as president of the Association for Psychological Type-Southeast.

Her recent publications include "Model Programs for Adult Learners in Higher Education," *Phi Delta Kappan*; "Comprehensive Counseling and Support Programs: Challenge to Higher Education," *New Perspectives on Counseling Adults*; and "The Myers-Briggs Type Indicator: A Tool for Appreciating Employee and Client Diversity," *Journal of Employment Counseling*.

INABETH MILLER holds a B.A. from Brown University, a M.S. from Simmons College, and an Ed.D. from Boston University. She has been a consultant to schools and corporations, particularly in the areas of libraries and the educational applications of interactive technologies. While serving as the librarian to the faculty of education, Harvard Graduate School of Education, she initiated nine conferences on educational issues, and published an on-line directory of school microcomputer use. She is presently the head of the Educational Technology and Outreach Activities at the Boston Museum of Science.

FAITH A. SANDLER currently serves as associate director for research and planning for the court-appointed Committee on Quality Education in St. Louis, Missouri. As part of the metropolitan St. Louis school desegregation effort, the committee evaluates aspects of the remedy designed to improve the system's all-black schools.

Originally from St. Louis, Ms. Sandler received her bachelor's degree from Johnston College in Redlands, California. In 1984 she received her master's degree in cultural anthropology from Washington University in St. Louis.

GAIL E. THOMAS received her Ph.D. from the University of North Carolina at Chapel Hill and is professor of sociology at Texas A & M University. Her main fields of interest are in race and sex differences in educational access and attainment, and stratification and institutional processes that impact the attainment outcomes of minorities. Dr. Thomas is currently engaged in research on race and sex interactions impacting students' college majors and career orientations; and institutional practices in recruiting and retaining minorities in various educational programs. She serves on a variety of national committees and task forces designed to address the problems and monitor the progress of minorities in higher education.

JOHN B. WILLIAMS is a lecturer on education and assistant to the president at Harvard University. He holds overall responsibility for affirmative action and equal employment opportunity programs at the university. He also teaches courses and conducts research on the politics of education, government regulation of higher education, public policy implementation, and urban education. Mr. Williams has taught at Vanderbilt University and has held a variety of positions in state and federal government. For several years he conducted community-based projects aimed at improving urban schools in New Jersey.

Mr. Williams earned his doctoral degree in education administration and policy analysis at Harvard. He earned his undergraduate degree at Princeton.

CHARLES V. WILLIE is a graduate of Morehouse College and Atlanta University with B.A. and M.A. degrees, respectively. His Ph.D. degree was awarded by Syracuse University in 1957. He has served as professor and chair of the Department of Sociology and as vice president of Syracuse University. Since 1974, he has been a faculty member of Harvard University's Graduate School of Education. A former president of the Eastern Sociological Society, he has been a member of the Council of the American Sociological Association and of the Board of Directors of the Social Science Research Council. President Jimmy Carter appointed him to the President's Commission on Mental Health. He has served as a court-appointed master, expert witness, and planning consultant for school desegregation in several cities and has written *School Desegregation Plans That Work, Effective Education,* and *The Ivory and Ebony Towers.*

ROBERT WIMPELBERG, Ph.D., is an associate professor and coordinator of the Educational Administration Program in the Department of Educational Leadership and Foundations at the University of New Orleans. His research interests include school reform and the work of school principals. Dr. Wimpelberg has served as editor of the *Administrator's Notebook* and is the treasurer of the Politics of Education Association. He completed his doctoral work in adminstrative, institutional, and policy studies in education at the University of Chicago.